Antietam

D0064098

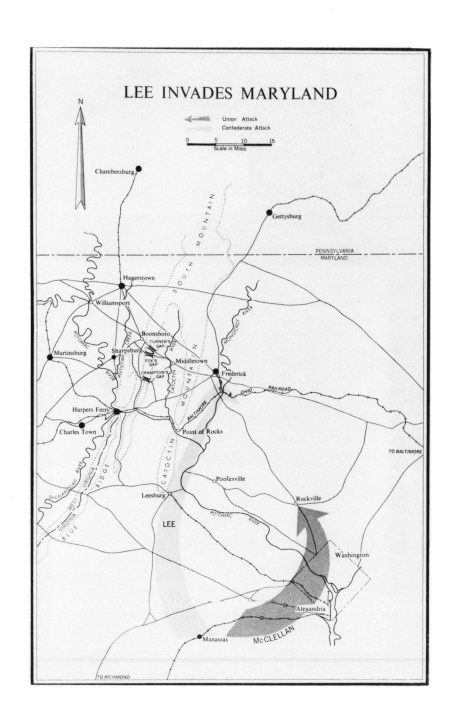

LEE INVADES MARYLAND

N

Union Attack
Confederate Attack

0   5   10   15
Scale in Miles

Chambersburg

Gettysburg

PENNSYLVANIA
MARYLAND

SOUTH MOUNTAIN

Hagerstown

Williamsport

MONOCACY RIVER

Boonsboro
TURNER'S GAP
FOX'S GAP
Middletown
CRAMPTON'S GAP

Martinsburg

Sharpsburg

ANTIETAM CREEK

POTOMAC RIVER

Frederick

OHIO   RAILROAD

BALTIMORE

CATOCTIN MOUNTAIN

Harpers Ferry

Point of Rocks

Charles Town

TO BALTIMORE

SHENANDOAH RIVER

WEST VIRGINIA

BLUE RIDGE

CATOCTIN

Poolesville

Leesburg

Rockville

POTOMAC   RIVER

LEE

Washington

Alexandria

McCLELLAN

Manassas

TO RICHMOND

Antietam

Essays on the 1862 Maryland Campaign

Edited by
Gary W. Gallagher

THE KENT STATE UNIVERSITY PRESS
Kent, Ohio, and London, England

© 1989 by The Kent State University Press, Kent, Ohio 44242
All rights reserved
Library of Congress Catalog Card Number 89-33453
ISBN 0-87338-399-0
ISBN 0-87338-400-8 (pbk.)
Manufactured in the United States of America

Library of Congress Cataloging-in-Publication Data

Antietam: essays on the 1862 Maryland campaign/edited by Gary W. Gallagher

    p.   cm.
    Bibliography: p.
    Includes index.
    ISBN 0-87338-399-0. —ISBN 0-87338-400-8 (pbk.)
1. Maryland Campaign, 1862—Congresses.   2. Antietam, Battle of,
1862—Congresses. I. Gallagher, Gary W.
E474.61.A58   1989
973.7'336—dc20   89-33453
                                               CIP

British Library Cataloging-in-Publication data are available.

973.7336
A629

Contents

Introduction

Students of the Civil War have long debated the relative importance of various military campaigns. Most attention has focused on the early summer of 1863, when Union armies won spectacular victories at Vicksburg and Gettysburg, and the fall of 1862, when Southern armies mounted simultaneous offensives into Maryland and Kentucky. Gettysburg achieved early and enduring *popular* acclaim as the single decisive moment. A range of factors explains Gettysburg's primacy, among them its sheer magnitude, the fact that the battle occurred on Northern soil, the importance of the climactic assault on July 3 as a symbolic "High Water Mark of the Confederacy," and Abraham Lincoln's eloquent benediction over the graves of Union dead. The number of monuments at Gettysburg, as well as the crush of tourists at the battlefield park, testify to the battle's hold on the American imagination.

Others have argued that Antietam rather than Gettysburg deserves recognition as the dividing line where Confederate fortunes shifted irrevocably toward defeat. Advocates of this view insist that never were so many political, diplomatic, and military elements aligned so favorably for the Confederacy. A victory in the hills of western Maryland or in southern Pennsylvania might well have propelled the South toward independence, but Lee's retreat after the ferocious bloodletting at Antietam changed everything, causing Europe to back away from recognition and opening the door for emancipation and its vast consequences. Certainly no other battle exceeded the drama and tragedy of Antietam. Across more than two centuries of the nation's involvement in wars of all kinds, Antietam remains the worst one-day slaughter in American history. The ghastly losses in the Cornfield, the West Woods, and the Sunken Road, the specter of the Confederacy's premier army courting absolute disaster while pinned against the Potomac River, and the inexplicable refusal of the Federal commander to press his advantage supply powerfully haunting images.

Central to the campaign was a memorable military and psychological confrontation between Robert E. Lee and George Brinton McClellan. Interestingly, the respective leaders each occupied a somewhat uncertain position in his army. Just three months had passed since Lee took charge of the Army of Northern Virginia following Joseph E. Johnston's wounding at the battle of Seven Pines. In that time he had restructured the army, won impressive victories during the Seven Days and at Second Manassas, and taken his soldiers across the Potomac in a raid predicated largely on logistics. Despite Lee's successes, however, he had not yet made the army his own; indeed, he operated in Maryland as a gifted and audacious stand-in pending Johnston's recovery. McClellan's situation was considerably more tenuous. Relegated to a secondary role in Washington because of his failure on the Peninsula, he had been restored to field command in the critical days after Second Manassas. His genius at organization quickly brought order out of chaos, but he knew that Lincoln and the Republicans in Congress had little faith in him. Believing that any mistake might provide ammunition for political enemies to take his beloved Army of the Potomac away from him, McClellan moved with great caution, his attention divided between the need to counter the aggressive Lee and a desire for self-preservation.

Much recent sentiment concedes the dramatic nature of contests such as that between Lee and McClellan but plays down the importance of all military activity during the war. Although prodigiously wasteful of human life, say those who subscribe to this interpretation, none of the great battles really decided much. Civil War armies were simply incapable of dealing knockout blows, with the consequence that they usually grappled for a brief deadly moment before predictably withdrawing to prepare for the next confrontation. Influenced to a considerable degree by the frustrating American experience in Vietnam, this approach calls into question the value of the close study of Civil War campaigns. James M. McPherson's *Battle Cry of Freedom* (New York, 1988), in contrast, reaffirms the importance of armies and campaigns, isolating four critical times during the war when military events "defined the eventual outcome." McPherson's quartet of turning points came in the summer of 1862 (Southern counteroffensives stopped the tide of Union success in the East and West), the autumn of 1862 (Northern armies repulsed Southern invasions at Antietam and Perryville), the summer of 1863 (Union victories at Gettysburg, Vicksburg, and Chattanooga turned the tide toward final Northern victory), and the late summer of 1864 (Sherman's success at Atlanta reversed growing Northern sentiment for a negotiated peace).

A debate thus continues on two levels. Were Civil War military campaigns important? And if so, what operations had the largest bearing on the course of the struggle? The essays below grew out of a conference on the Maryland campaign of 1862 held at the Mont Alto Campus of Pennsylvania State University in June 1988. The conference itself originated from a belief that the military events of late summer and fall 1862 *were* important, perhaps decisive. The authors sought to address a number of questions about the origins, conduct, and outcome of the campaign. Was Lee's movement across the Potomac strategically sound? Did the Confederates have a reasonable chance of success? How did the leadership of each army perform? What were the critical moments of the campaign? What was the short- and long-term impact of the campaign?

These five brief essays make no claim to definitive answers. They are often speculative, and the authors, as readers will quickly discover, sometimes disagree. If the essays inspire some individuals to explore in more depth the 1862 Maryland campaign, or to think about some of its facets in new ways, they will have achieved their primary purpose.

Working with Bob Krick, Will Greene, and Dennis Frye at the Mont Alto conference and in putting this book together was a pleasure. Each of them combines in refreshing proportion enthusiasm, knowledge of their subjects, and a respect for deadlines. Eileen Anne Gallagher typed most of the manuscript, made her usual accurate suggestions for tightening prose, and gently encouraged me to use Sharpsburg rather than Antietam wherever possible. I thank them all for their humor and help with this project.

GARY W. GALLAGHER

The Autumn of 1862
A Season of Opportunity

White's Ford on the Potomac River near Leesburg, Virginia, presented a memorable scene on September 4–7, 1862. The weather was brilliantly fine, with bright sunshine playing off the water of the historic river that symbolized the division between North and South. Wildflowers grew thickly along the banks, their vivid colors standing out against dense foliage of towering trees that framed the Potomac. Long lines of veterans of the Confederate Army of Northern Virginia, victors in recent battles with the Army of the Potomac outside Richmond and on the rolling plains of Manassas, made their way across the river into Maryland. Above the winding columns, the careless chatter of soldiers mixed with strains of ''Maryland, My Maryland'' played by Confederate bands on the east side of the Potomac. It was a grand panorama of an army in motion, only slightly flawed by the obviously ragged appearance of the Southern soldiers.

The Confederacy's leadership sensed opportunity in late summer and early autumn 1862. As R. E. Lee's soldiers tramped into Maryland, Southern fortunes on the battlefield rapidly approached their crest. Far to the west, forces under Generals Braxton Bragg and Edmund Kirby Smith soon would move into the bluegrass region of Kentucky—between them, the raids into Maryland and Kentucky would mark the high point of the South's military effort. Lee and the Army of Northern Virginia shouldered the principal burden of making this great Southern counteroffensive a success. While it is true that in a strictly military sense the war would be won in the western theater, where Ulysses S. Grant, William Tecumseh Sherman, and George H. Thomas eventually overmatched their Confederate opponents, many people *perceived* the eastern theater to be the critical arena. Much of the Northern and Southern public, important politicians on both sides, and foreign observers and governments focused on the well-traveled one hundred-mile strip of disputed land between Washington

Army of Northern Virginia Crossing at White's Ford on the Potomac

and Richmond for signs of victory. The opposing capitals were there, the most famous armies were there—the war must be decided there.

Abraham Lincoln found the tendency of his fellow countrymen to concentrate on the Virginia theater very frustrating. He had decided quite early that the West was the crucial geographical region, yet most Northerners failed to grasp this fact. That failure stood in stark relief in early summer 1862 when the North plunged into gloom over George B. McClellan's inability to capture Richmond during the Seven Days campaign. Lee had not beaten the Army of the Potomac, had not even driven it from the Peninsula below Richmond, yet most people interpreted McClellan's campaign as an utter fiasco. Lincoln commented on this phenomenon in a letter of August 4, 1862, to French Count Agénor-Etienne de Gasparin: "The moral effect was the worst of the failure before Richmond. . . . I believe it is true that in men and material, the enemy suffered more than we." In answering Gasparin's call for more victories (by which he clearly meant victories in the East), Lincoln alluded to the lack of Northern appreciation of the Federal triumphs at Forts Henry and Donelson, Shiloh, Nashville, and New Orleans: "It seems unreasonable that a series of successes, extending through half-a-year, and clearing more than a hundred thousand square miles of country, should help us so little, while a single half-defeat should hurt us so much.'' Although certainly unreasonable, this eastern bias was a reality that made Lee's movements loom all the larger in September 1862.

A combination of diplomatic, political, and military factors formed an equation of potential opportunity for the Confederacy in the fall of 1862. The governments of England and France watched events with special interest. The London *Times* set the tone for many in Britain when it observed that the Seven Days, which it called a severe Union defeat, had been one of the epochal battles of the century. ''After pouring forth blood like water and fertilizing the fields of Virginia with thousands of corpses,'' stated the *Times* in late July, ''the North finds itself obliged to begin all over again, with credit destroyed, a ruined revenue, a depreciated currency, and an enormous debt.'' A firm believer that the South must demonstrate its independence before Britain intervened as an arbitrator, Prime Minister Viscount Palmerston overlooked Federal activities west of the Appalachians and interpreted the Seven Days as a turning point. He wrote the queen on August 6 that England should propose an armistice in October, when the results of the fall campaigning in Virginia presumably would be known (and presumably would favor the South).

Lee's victory at Second Manassas on August 29–30 added to the expectation of probable Northern failure. Palmerston thought General John Pope's Army of Virginia had gotten a ''very complete smashing'' that placed at risk Washington and Baltimore, while Lord John Russell, who as head of the Foreign Office had resisted British interference in the American upheaval, concluded that Lee's movement north presaged an end to the war. By mid-September (it took news at least ten days to travel from America to England), Palmerston spoke of Britain and France proffering ''an arrangement upon the basis of separation'' between the warring sections. Chancellor of the Exchequer William Gladstone favored outright recognition of the Confederacy; in these three men, the South had powerful supporters who might sway a cabinet that contained several members devoted to strict neutrality. The English people were divided on the question. Historians long thought class governed British attitudes toward the American war, with working-class, antislavery sentiment for the Union and aristocratic, privileged classes for the slaveholding Confederacy. In fact, economic self-interest blurred class lines. So long as the North did not declare emancipation a war aim, the pervasive abolitionist impulse in England would not coalesce behind the Lincoln government.

Emperor Louis Napoleon of France waited for England to make the first move. Confederate independence would abet his scheme to create a vassal state in Mexico and bring more cotton to French ports, but after the Russians declined a French suggestion for Anglo-French-Russian mediation in late July 1862 the emperor decided that British action was vital. French Foreign Minister Antoine Edouard Thouvenel averred in late summer that no ''reasonable statesman in Europe'' doubted that the Confederacy would win the war. French minister to the United States Baron Henri Mercier advised his superiors in Paris on September 2 that Union setbacks during the Seven Days and at Second Manassas had created an atmosphere conducive to mediation in the North. On September 17, the day of the battle of Antietam, Lord Russell agreed with Palmerston that Britain should offer to mediate ''with a view to the recognition of the independence of the Confederates.'' Should such mediation fail, added Russell, ''we ought ourselves to recognize the Southern States as an independent State.'' He concluded with the observation that a Federal defeat in Maryland would prepare the North to receive Britain's proposal.

Confederate representatives in Europe predicted as early as the end of July that recognition was imminent. In Liverpool, United States Consul Thomas Dudley seconded this reading of events when he stated on July 19 that all of Europe was against the North and ''would rejoice at our downfall.'' Lee and his army held the key to diplomatic movement on the Continent. Another win for the Army of Northern Virginia might well bring recognition for the Confederacy. In their optimism, Southerners thought back to the alliance with France in 1778 and the French ships and soldiers that tipped the scales in favor of George Washington's army at Yorktown. But parallels between 1778 and 1862 were flawed. European military intervention on the side of the Confederacy was highly unlikely; moreover, the Lincoln administration left no doubt that despite any setback on the battlefield it would rebuff mediation. In sum, a diplomatic opportunity of unknown magnitude hung tantalizingly before the Confederacy in September 1862.

It seemed also within the reach of Southern arms to influence Northern politics. The Lincoln administration anticipated determined opposition from Democrats on a range of issues in the summer and fall of 1862; unless Federal armies produced victories in the autumn campaigns the Republicans stood to suffer in the November off-year elections. Apart from their long-standing differences with the Republicans over economic issues, Democrats argued that draconian measures such as Lincoln's selective suspension of the writ of habeas corpus mocked individual rights. They resented the Militia Act of July 17, 1862, which gave the president broad powers to coerce service in federal militia units. They blanched when Lincoln, facing a severe shortage of men, issued a call for three hundred thousand nine-month militiamen in the first week of August, and the War Department sent instructions on enrollment and draft procedures to the states.

Perhaps most galling to the Democrats was increasing pressure from many Republicans to add emancipation as a Northern objective. The war had changed, insisted outraged Democrats. They supported a war to preserve the Union and its constitutional safeguards for citizens' rights, but the conflict had become a gross distortion of that original crusade. Unbridled federal power had grown arrogant and oppressive, threatening to compel whites to die for the freedom of blacks. Northern Democrats expressed their unhappiness and frustration in words and, increasingly, with acts of violence.

The extent of antiwar sentiment north of the Potomac was well known but imperfectly understood in the Confederacy. Jefferson Davis and R. E. Lee read newspaper accounts of a developing peace party. Lee thought the presence of his army north of the Potomac for several weeks in the fall of 1862 would galvanize Northern opposition to the war. Five days after the first of his infantry had crossed the Potomac at White's Ford, he wrote Davis that the time seemed propitious for the Confederacy to suggest that the United States recognize its independence. More than a year of fighting had brought intense suffering "without advancing the objects which our enemies proposed to themselves in beginning the contest." "The rejection of this offer would prove to the country that the responsibility of the continuance of the war does not rest upon us," reasoned Lee, "but that the party in power in the United States elect to prosecute it for purposes of their own." In offering peace, the South could "enable the people of the United States to determine at their coming elections whether they will support those who favor a prolongation of the war, or those who wish to bring it to a termination, which can but be productive of good to both parties without affecting the honor of either."

Lee and Davis held high hopes for the state of Maryland. Had not that slave state been kept in the Union by Federal bayonets? In April 1861 citizens of Baltimore had rioted against the 6th Massachusetts Regiment. Marylanders had been arrested and incarcerated without benefit of the writ of habeas corpus. Thirty-one secessionist members of the state legislature, together with the mayor of Baltimore, had been imprisoned for several weeks during the fall of 1861. Similar heavy-handed measures had ensured a unionist majority in the legislature elected in November 1861. Some Marylanders arrested on political grounds still languished in prison when the Army of Northern Virginia entered the state; neither they nor any of those released earlier had seen any evidence against them. "In no case has an arrest been made on mere suspicion," Lincoln had stated in September 1861, ". . . but in all cases the Government is in possession of tangible and unmistakable evidence, which will, when made public, be satisfactory to every loyal citizen." The president's words rang hollow to thousands of Marylanders who wondered if their liberties would stand in abeyance for the duration of the war. Lee thought the influence of his victorious army might embolden citizens of Maryland to step forward in active support of the Confederacy, after which they could once again "enjoy the inalienable rights of freemen, and restore independence and sovereignty to your State."

Lee and Davis were correct in assuming that a Southern victory or a protracted stay north of the Potomac would hurt the Republicans in November. They went too far, however, in thinking that even a resounding Democratic victory would bring Northern recognition of Confederate independence. They

General Robert E. Lee

confused Democratic unhappiness with the direction of the war with sentiment receptive to disunion. Only extreme Democrats countenanced the notion of a sovereign Confederacy; most were devoted to a conservative prosecution of the conflict embodied in the slogan "The Constitution as it is, the Union as it was." Lee and Davis similarly misread Maryland (Bragg and Kirby Smith made the same mistake in Kentucky), for the western part of the state, through which the Army of Northern Virginia passed, was staunchly unionist. The eastern shore and Baltimore held most of Maryland's secessionists, who were far from the liberating influence of Lee's forces. Success on the battlefield in Maryland probably would have earned few recruits for Lee's army. More important, Democratic political gains triggered by such a victory almost certainly would not have led to mediation of the question of Southern independence. Confederate opportunity to affect Northern politics through military success thus was limited to influencing *how* rather than *if* the North would continue to wage the war for the Union.

The resolution of one momentous issue did depend largely on the outcome of Lee's raid into Maryland. Lincoln had decided in midsummer to issue a proclamation of emancipation. Pressed by elements of his party to move more quickly, and weary of obstinate refusals by the Border States to consider any type of emancipation, Lincoln had announced his intention to the cabinet on July 22. Debate among his advisers convinced the president to hold off until the North won a military victory; otherwise, as Secretary of State William H. Seward said, the proclamation would appear to be "the last measure of an exhausted government, a cry for help." Once issued, Lincoln's proclamation would alter the nature of the war, making it a struggle for freedom as well as for restoration of the Union. Northern victory would cost the South its slaves, thereby shattering its social and economic fabric. The proclamation also would render it nearly impossible for Britain, which had abolished slavery in the 1830s, to support a slave-based Confederacy against a North fighting for emancipation. Ironically, Lee knew nothing of his chance to influence Lincoln's course on emancipation, though it was potentially the most profound of the opportunities present in the autumn of 1862.

Politics and diplomacy figured in Lee's conception of what his army might accomplish across the Potomac, but his principal goals were military. John Pope's Army of Virginia and George B. McClellan's Army of the Potomac lay "weakened and demoralized" in the vicinity of Washington. That presented an opportunity to flank the Federal capital by marching into Maryland. This would not be an invasion—Lee had no intention of holding any Union territory indefinitely—but a great raid during which the Confederates would maintain a flanking posture northwest of Washington for most if not all of the fall season. Such a course offered diverse potential value. The Federals would have to position themselves north of the Potomac to guard Washington, thereby freeing northern Virginia of contending armies and allowing the Confederates to strengthen the defenses of Richmond. Lee would hold the initiative in Maryland, whereas in Virginia he could do little more than wait for the next Union effort to turn his position and strike at the Southern capital. The raid would bring desperately needed supplies from Maryland and perhaps Pennsylvania to the Army of Northern Virginia. At the same time, the fall harvest in the Shenandoah Valley and elsewhere in Virginia might be gathered in safety. When the approach of winter exhausted supplies in Maryland, Lee would withdraw to Virginia.

Lee expressed no fear of aggressive Union reaction to his raid. Reports through the first week of September indicated that the Federals were concentrating in their fortifications at Washington and Alexandria. Should a Northern force stir itself to press Lee, he would have the advantage of fighting on the tactical defensive in a place of his choosing. ''The only two subjects that give me any uneasiness,'' Lee wrote Davis on September 4, ''are my supplies of ammunition and subsistence.'' The former was not an immediate problem: ''I have enough for present use, and must await results before deciding to what point I will have additional supplies forwarded.'' The farms of western Maryland would answer needs for food and fodder. Lee summed up his analysis of the military, political, and diplomatic opportunities of early autumn 1862 in the opening sentence of a letter to Davis on September 3: ''The present seems to be the most propitious time since the commencement of the war for the Confederate Army to enter Maryland.''

Lee manifestly believed he could take advantage of at least some of the opportunities that beckoned. But was his army equipped to carry out a major campaign across the Potomac in early September 1862? If it was not, the glimmering possibilities at home and abroad were but so many dancing mirages. Most writers have proceeded from the assumption that the South could have attained more if only certain crucial episodes had gone differently—if, for example, Lee's orders for the campaign had not fallen into McClellan's hands on September 13. A close look at the Army of Northern Virginia as it entered and maneuvered in Maryland during the first ten days of the raid—before any fighting took place— suggests otherwise.

The numerical strength of the Army of Northern Virginia on the eve of the campaign was at best marginally adequate to undertake an operation that might result in battle against Federal forces approaching one hundred thousand soldiers. Two months of hard fighting and marching had extracted a grievous toll. One careful observer wrote that when the army was at Frederick, Maryland, on September 7 its ''divisions had sunk to little more than brigades, & brigades nearly to regiments.'' Though impossible to estimate with precision, Lee's effectives at the time he crossed the river probably totaled 40,000 to 45,000 infantry, 5,500 cavalry, and 4,000 artillery—in all, 50,000 to 55,000 men. Critical shortages of clothing and equipment added to a grim situation. Lee himself admitted to Davis on September 3 that "the army is not properly equipped for an invasion of an enemy's territory." "It lacks much of the material of war," Lee stated, "is feeble in transportation, the animals being much reduced, and the men are poorly provided with clothes, and in thousands of instances are destitute of shoes." This sobering information appeared in the same letter wherein Lee told Davis it was "the most propitious time since the commencement of the war" to carry the war northward. With scarcely half the men and but a fraction of the material resources of his foe, Lee could expect very little margin for error in Maryland.

Lee could look with assurance to his principal subordinates. James Longstreet and Stonewall Jackson had matured in the crucible of fighting on the Peninsula and during the campaign of Second Manassas. Together with Lee, they would do much to make the Army of Northern Virginia a formidable instrument—in time one of the legendary field commands. Although each was injured in early September, they could be relied upon for solid direction at the top. No less an asset was Jeb Stuart, whose skill in screening and reconnaissance and presence of mind on the battlefield assured Lee of superlative cavalry support. William Nelson Pendleton provided indifferent direction to the artillery, though able young subordinates substantially offset his ineptitude.

Lower levels of command presented a darker picture. Attrition among generals had been frightful since late June. Colonels led eight of Stonewall Jackson's fourteen brigades, and with Richard S. Ewell out of action because of his wound at Groveton and A. P. Hill under arrest due to a dispute with Jackson, not one of his divisional commanders held the appropriate rank of major general. Longstreet's wing was in better shape, although John Bell Hood, Longstreet's fiercest fighter, was under arrest as a result of a silly quarrel with Brigadier General Nathan "Shanks" Evans over some ambulances captured at Second Manassas. Losses among field and company grade officers in both Jackson's and Longstreet's wings had been so high since June that efficiency and discipline suffered serious declines.

Lee's emphasis on the need to provision his army in Maryland told the story of food and fodder in the Army of Northern Virginia. Men and animals alike suffered cruel shortages. Testimony on this point is so overwhelming and well known that a single example will suffice to convey the gravity of Lee's plight. A soldier in James L. Kemper's brigade of D. R. Jones's division remembered that as the army turned north on September 2 after the battle of Chantilly, "[our] haversacks were all turned wrong side out and the very dust of the crackers were scraped out and devoured." The next day there was "still no sign of our commissary wagons, and not a mouthful of food did we have all day." September 4 brought some green corn, and for three days the soldiers relied on that bowel-churning fare. On September 8 this soldier wrote simply, "[W]e are hungry, for six days not a morsel of bread or meat had gone into our stomachs—and our menu consisted of apples and corn.'' Horses and mules were in a similar state. The lack of shoes among Lee's men posed another barrier to effective maneuver. A soldier from Georgia put this crisis very succinctly: ''I had no shoes. I tried it barefoot, but somehow my feet wouldn't callous. They just kept bleeding.'' Try as he might, this man could not keep up with his unit.

In ragged clothing, poorly shod, and inadequately nourished, the men of the Army of Northern Virginia, as well as the animals that toiled alongside them, were not physically prepared for an active raid into Maryland and Pennsylvania. And Lee's admission of as much on September 3 did not portend a successful campaign.

The morale of the Army of Northern Virginia as it embarked on its raid deserves closer scrutiny than it has received from historians. Nearly every writer dwells on the massive amount of straggling. An army that crossed the Potomac with 50,000 to 55,000 men mustered fewer than 40,000 bayonets at Sharpsburg on September 17. The loss of so many of his men chastened Lee. ''Our great embarrassment,'' he wrote Davis on September 13, ''is the reduction in our ranks by straggling, which it seems impossible to prevent with our present regimental officers. Our ranks are much diminished—I fear from a third to one-half of the original number.'' Alexander Cheves Haskell, member of a South Carolina family that sent seven brothers into the Confederate army, wrote home just after Antietam that, ''Our army is small, but fights gloriously. . . . Great numbers of men have straggled off, until none but heroes are left.'' Young Brigadier General William Dorsey Pender of A. P. Hill's division noted in exasperation on September 19: ''In one of my regt's the other day. . . six out of 10 officers skulked out. . . . More than half my brigade went off the same day. Oh dear, oh dear, our army is coming to a pretty pass.'' Stern warnings, hangings (especially in Jackson's command), and other harsh measures failed to stop the flood of soldiers dropping away from their units.

What had happened? Why did the army, following two resounding victories, hemorrhage at such an alarming rate? The traditional explanations are familiar: thousands of men fell out of the ranks because their unshod feet gave out; malnourishment and diarrhea left others too weak to carry on; others still, especially those from western North Carolina, felt uncomfortable moving north to fight on enemy soil (they had enlisted to defend their homes). All of these men, the usual argument goes, rejoined their units as soon as the army returned to Virginia.

Taken as a group, these factors undoubtedly account for a large percentage of the men who were not present at Antietam. They do not, however, explain the phenomenon of Lee's losing fully one-third of his army. Lee himself admitted to Davis on September 21 (when the army was back in Virginia) that his force ''remained greatly paralyzed by the loss to its ranks of many stragglers. I have taken every means in my power from the beginning to correct this evil, which has increased rather than diminished.'' Many soldiers never entered Maryland, stated Lee, while others who did move north "kept aloof." "The stream has not lessened since crossing the Potomac [recrossing the river back into Virginia]," Lee concluded, "though the cavalry has been constantly employed in suppressing it." What Lee described was more than straggling—it was straggling in tandem with large-scale desertion. Desertion is an ugly word that few who have studied the Maryland campaign have been willing to use, but desertion it was that kept men away from their units *during* and *after* the campaign.

Lee also acknowledged that his soldiers were plundering beyond the control of their officers. Although he devoted considerable time to stopping this wanton destruction of private property, Lee confessed to Davis that he was having little success. General John R. Jones, who was assigned to round up those absent from their commands, reported ten days after Antietam that he had sent approximately six thousand back to the army, but that the area around Winchester was still "full of stragglers." "Many of them have deliberately thrown away their shoes so they would have an excuse for being away," said Jones in disgust, and the "number of officers back here was most astonishing." This shocking situation indicated more than a lack of sufficient food and shoes. Clearly, an unprecedented percentage of the Army of Northern Virginia suffered from low morale and lax discipline and simply refused to fight in Maryland. Alexander Haskell's comment was most revealing—the steadfast heroes fought magnificently at Antietam, but they fought without the help of thousands of their compatriots.

The loss of veteran company and field grade officers doubtless contributed to poor discipline and morale during the Maryland campaign. The wearing toll of more than two months of strenuous marching punctuated by heavy combat also played a role. William Garrett Piston has suggested that the shift from Joseph E. Johnston's to Lee's leadership may have been a third factor. Many soldiers in the army considered Lee a stand-in for the popular Johnston, who, they believed, would return following his recuperation. By the first of September, some of these men may have seen all they wanted of Lee's style of generalship. In three months under Lee's direction, the army had suffered more than thirty-five thousand battle casualties (Antietam would add another ten thousand). This was bloodshed on an unimaginable scale; it might have fostered feelings among some of the men that if they survived until Johnston resumed command they had a better chance of living a full life. Whatever the complete story of the straggling and desertion in the Army of Northern Virginia, it seems incontrovertible that morale and discipline were uneven. Lee did not go north with an army that had the self-confidence, devotion to its commander, and profound willingness to do anything asked of it that would be its trademark in another few months.

Because of these problems and the material odds against them, Lee and his army probably lacked the capacity to achieve a decisive victory or maintain a protracted presence in the North. Porter Alexander, who was perhaps the most astute of all the Confederates who wrote about the war, argued that in light of inferior Southern strength and supplies, "a drawn battle, such as we did actually fight, was the best *possible* outcome one could hope for." Only McClellan's unbelievable timidity and failure to fight his entire army, added Alexander, permitted even that unsatisfactory result. Barring egregious errors or criminal sloth on the part of his opponent, Lee's army reasonably stood scant chance of seizing the political, diplomatic, and military opportunities that have fascinated students of the Maryland campaign.

The real opportunity that autumn lay in Federal hands. Confronted with a range of potential rewards, the audacious Lee had calculated the risks and chosen to go north. He relied on a period of Federal confusion and inaction after Second Manassas to permit his establishment of a good position in Maryland before having to confront any menace from the Army of the Potomac. But Lee underestimated George B. McClellan's brilliance in rallying Pope's dispirited troops. Within days McClellan restored morale and built confidence among the ranks of his combined force, and Lincoln discerned that a beautiful opening lay before the Federals. Lee's army was vulnerable once it had crossed into Maryland, its safe passage to Virginia dependent on the Potomac's fords. The farther north Lee went, thought Lincoln, the more tenuous his position. Unaffected by the hysteria that gripped much of the North following news of the Confederate raid, Lincoln concentrated on offensive operations. Receiving reports on September 12 that the enemy was crossing back into Virginia, he urged McClellan, "Please do not let him get off without being hurt." Three days later the president implored his general to "destroy the rebel army, if possible."

Lincoln's hopes were not fanciful. The fall of 1862 was the only time in the war that one major army in the East had an opportunity to destroy another major army. Many generals loved to talk about fashioning Cannae-type victories, but McClellan actually had such an opportunity in mid-September 1862 with Lee's outnumbered army backed against the Potomac at Sharpsburg. When Lee decided to stay north of the Potomac and offer battle, he gave McClellan the most incredible military opportunity of the conflict. Porter Alexander termed Lee's action the greatest blunder he ever committed and marveled at McClellan's good fortune: "Not twice in a lifetime does such a chance come to any general. Lee for once has made a mistake, & given you a chance to ruin him if you can break his lines, & such game is worth great risks."

Great risks and great opportunities were the leitmotifs of the 1862 Maryland campaign. Willing to risk all in pursuit of opportunities he and his government saw before them, Lee misjudged the resources of his army. That miscalculation thrust before the Federals a most dazzling opportunity for which McClellan, despite Lincoln's prodding and the fortuitous capture of Lee's plans, declined to risk anything. The stakes in September 1862 were as high as they ever got in a war that would drag on for another two and a half years. The campaign in Maryland, with its horrific climax at Antietam, did much to determine the outcome of that mighty struggle.

Major General George Brinton McClellan

DENNIS E. FRYE

Drama between the Rivers

Harpers Ferry in the 1862 Maryland Campaign

Robert E. Lee's plan to capture Harpers Ferry, Virginia, in September 1862 was audacious. He would split his army into four parts, scattering them across the points of the compass and sending three widely separated columns against the Federal stronghold at the confluence of the Shenandoah and Potomac rivers. The Confederates converging on Harpers Ferry would have just three days to seize high ground to the east, south, and west of the town (coordinating their movements with signal flags), trap the enemy, bombard the defenses, force a surrender, remove captured booty, and march quickly northward to reunite with the rest of the Army of Northern Virginia at a predetermined point.

James Longstreet argued against the ambitious blueprint. "I thought it a venture not worth the game," remembered Lee's wing commander after the war, "and suggested, as we were in the enemy's country and presence, that he would be advised of any move that we made in a few hours...that...if they found us exposed, [they could] make serious trouble before the capture could be accomplished." Stonewall Jackson, who commanded Lee's other wing, accepted the logistical challenge. He pronounced the plan practicable and expressed satisfaction at the prospect of returning to the Shenandoah Valley, especially since he lately had neglected his Federal friends there. Lee replied that these "friends" would not be happy to see the famous but dreaded Stonewall.

With his principal lieutenants offering contradictory advice, Lee contemplated his next move. Nearly fourteen thousand Union soldiers garrisoned the lower Shenandoah Valley, posing a serious threat to Confederate lines of communications and supply. The Army of Northern Virginia had crossed into Maryland between September 4–7, a maneuver Lee had expected would prompt the Federals to withdraw from the valley. But the Union troops remained steadfastly in place at Harpers Ferry and Martinsburg, disrupting Lee's freedom of movement. Something had to be done.

Lee reached his final decision on September 9 while resting his army near Frederick. He would divide the army into four parts. Three columns would march upon Harpers Ferry; General Jackson would command this three-pronged pincer movement while the remainder of the army and its supply trains awaited the outcome at Boonsboro, twenty miles north of the Ferry. Lee allotted three days for completion of the operation—only three days. He labelled the plan Special Orders No. 191, and on the morning of September 10 the army began to execute it.

The primary hazard imperiling the scheme—getting caught before the operation ended—seemed not to bother the Confederate commander. Lee assessed his opponent, Major General George B. McClellan, as "an able general but a very cautious one," whose Army of the Potomac lay in Washington "in a very demoralized and chaotic condition," that would prevent its taking the offensive for three or four weeks. Lee thus expected his special orders to yield rapid and favorable results. But was his army, hungry and ragged and worn from two months of solid campaigning, equal to the task? Had Lee adequately considered the condition of his men in formulating Special Orders No. 191? Probably not, for the tired and foot-blistered columns heading for Harpers Ferry quickly fell behind schedule; as a result, Lee almost gambled his army into extinction.

While the Confederates tramped toward Harpers Ferry much more slowly than expected, McClellan organized his army with greater speed than Lee had anticipated. During the first week of September 1862, McClellan had transformed two demoralized Federal armies into a formidable force approaching ninety thousand men. "Again I have been called to save the country," McClellan wrote his wife shortly after the Confederates crossed the Potomac. "You don't know what a task has been imposed upon me! The case is desperate, but with God's help I will try unselfishly to do my best and accomplish the salvation of the nation."

Under orders to protect Baltimore and Washington and to block an invasion of Pennsylvania, McClellan—sensing the urgency to focus Lee in his sights, but bound by his innate caution—slowly moved the army northwest from the Federal capital. By September 13, Little Mac had arrived in Frederick, vacated three days before by Lee and his army. McClellan had voiced displeasure over maintaining the Federal garrison at Harpers Ferry before he departed Washington. As a stationary garrison, he thought, it was ripe for capture. McClellan recommended withdrawal of the troops north to Hagerstown, where they could contest a Confederate advance up the Cumberland Valley into Pennsylvania; however, General-in-Chief Henry W. Halleck overruled McClellan's suggestions for redeployment.

Old Brains Halleck (characterized by one observer as a man who "originates nothing, anticipates nothing. . . plans nothing, suggests nothing, [and] is good for nothing") considered the Harpers Ferry garrison most secure *at* Harpers

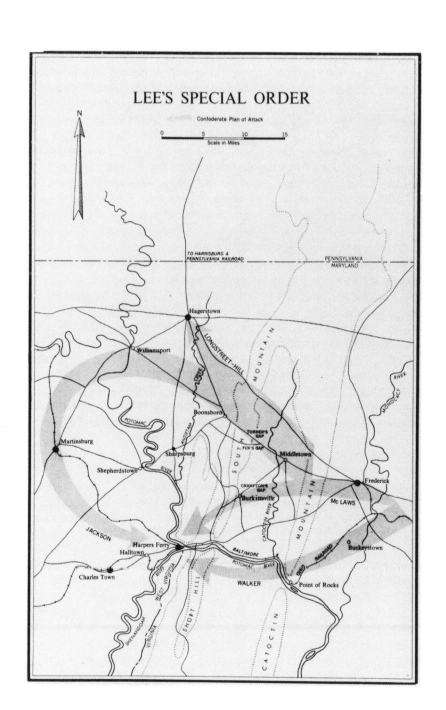

LEE'S SPECIAL ORDER

Confederate Plan of Attack

0   5   10   15
Scale in Miles

N

TO HARRISBURG &
PENNSYLVANIA RAILROAD

PENNSYLVANIA
MARYLAND

Hagerstown

Williamsport

LONGSTREET-HILL

Boonsboro

Martinsburg

Sharpsburg

Shepherdstown

TURNER'S GAP

FOX'S GAP

Middletown

CRAMPTON'S GAP

Burkittsville

Mc LAWS

Frederick

JACKSON

Harpers Ferry

Halltown

BALTIMORE

POTOMAC RIVER

RAILROAD

Buckeystown

Charles Town

WALKER

Point of Rocks

SHORT HILL

WEST VIRGINIA

SHENANDOAH RIVER

VIRGINIA

CATOCTIN

SOUTH MOUNTAIN

MOUNTAIN

CATOCTIN RIVER

MONOCACY RIVER

POTOMAC RIVER

ANTIETAM CREEK

Ferry. Halleck curiously reasoned that withdrawal from Harpers Ferry would "expose the garrison to capture" and force destruction of all artillery and stores collected at the site. He concluded that the only feasible plan called for retention of Harpers Ferry until McClellan could relieve it. At first glance Halleck's logic defies explanation, because holding the garrison at Harpers Ferry surely exposed it to capture. But keeping troops at Harpers Ferry forced Lee to deal with an enemy in his rear—a problem he did not expect. Halleck's tenacious grip on Harpers Ferry consequently compelled Lee to halt his advance north and redirect half of the Confederate army back toward the Potomac River. Halleck, in effect, stalled the Southern invasion.

Determination to hold Harpers Ferry at all hazards reflected Halleck's stubbornness. On September 5, 1862, one day after Lee crossed into Maryland, Colonel Dixon S. Miles, commander of the garrison at Harpers Ferry, received frantic orders to be "energetic and active, and defend all places to the last extremity. There must be no abandoning of a post, and shoot the first man that thinks of it." Several hours later the telegraph rattled again: "Have your wits about you, and do all you can to annoy the rebels should they advance on you. . . .You will not abandon Harper's Ferry without defending it to the last extremity."

These urgent messages perhaps reflected a lack of confidence in the fifty-eight-year-old Dixon Stansbury Miles. Although a West Pointer and forty-year veteran, Miles had seen his reputation tarnished at First Bull Run when another officer accused him of drunkenness. Although cleared of the charge by a court of inquiry, Miles witnessed former subordinates rise in rank and distinction in the Army of the Potomac while he remained on leave awaiting orders. An embittered Miles finally received command of the Railroad Brigade on March 29, 1862, and soon established his headquarters at Harpers Ferry to perform the duty of "protecting the line of the Baltimore and Ohio Railway."

Miles knew the Confederates were coming toward Harpers Ferry. Reports from his scouts on September 4 had sent the first alarms of invasion to Washington, and one week later his cavalry tracked the movements dictated by Special Orders No. 191 that sent three Southern columns closer and closer to the Federal garrison. Just before Lee issued 191, Miles wired his superiors, "I am ready for them."

In response to the Confederate threat, Miles divided his eleven-thousand-man garrison into four brigades. Two of the brigades, some seven thousand strong, took position along Bolivar Heights, a low-lying ridge that stretched a mile and a half from the Potomac on the north to the swiftly flowing Shenandoah on the south. Although two miles west of Harpers Ferry, Miles considered Bolivar Heights important because its abrupt three hundred-foot rise from the valley floor made it a formidable defensive position. A Confederate assault not only would require scaling the heights, but also traversing a half mile of open fields under Federal artillery and infantry fire. Miles believed an attack on Bolivar Heights would result in a slaughter of Confederates similar to that at Malvern

Hill some two months before. In support of his position on Bolivar Heights, Miles placed a one-thousand-man brigade of heavy artillery and accompanying infantry on Camp Hill, a geologic ''wart'' towering three hundred feet above the confluence of the Shenandoah and Potomac. The 20-pounder Parrotts on Camp Hill, which lay about a thousand yards west of Bolivar Heights, easily covered the principal Federal line.

The Bolivar Heights–Camp Hill combination shielded Harpers Ferry from attack from the west, but this defensive line would be untenable should the Confederates take two higher ridges surrounding the Ferry—Maryland Heights and Loudoun Heights. Maryland Heights dwarfed the other three mountains encircling the town. Its 1,460-foot elevation exceeded that of its nearest competitor (Loudoun Heights) by 500 feet, and Bolivar Heights and Camp Hill appeared as foothills in the shadow of the Maryland mountain. Miles realized he had to retain the highest ground, and he consequently assigned a brigade of two thousand infantry to defend the crest of Maryland Heights. Miles also positioned two 9-inch Dahlgrens and a 50-pounder rifle halfway up the southwest slope of Maryland Heights; from this Naval Battery the colonel expected long-range artillery support for the lines on Bolivar Heights and Camp Hill.

No Federals occupied Loudoun Heights because Miles considered it minimally important in the defense of Harpers Ferry. The Federal commander deemed the terrain on Loudoun Heights too rugged for enemy artillery, and experience had taught him that Confederate infantry could cause little harm from that distance. Moreover, Miles reasoned that a few well-directed shots from the Naval Battery could scatter an attacking force there.

Comfortable with his defensive lines, Colonel Miles nonetheless had doubts about his soldiers. Two weeks before Lee's invasion commenced, Miles had received trainloads of raw recruits at his Harpers Ferry headquarters. Many of these new faces were men from upstate New York who had just enlisted for three years' service. Miles declared the newcomers unfit, reporting on August 27 that they ''never had a gun in their hands until the boxes were opened and the muskets issued to them yesterday.'' Disdainful of the new men's leaders as well, Miles stated that they scarcely deserved to call themselves officers since they knew not ''how to drill or anything about the drill.'' The colonel bitterly complained to a superior that Harpers Ferry had become ''nothing more than a fortified camp of instruction.'' When Miles divided his force into four brigades on September 4, he attempted to obviate the problem of inexperience by placing at least one veteran regiment (and ninety-days' men qualified as ''veterans'') in each of the four. This arrangement doubtless provided little comfort, however, to a man soon to face ''the flower of Lee's army.''

Thus far, the flower and vine Robert E. Lee sent to Harpers Ferry on September 10 had failed to strangle Colonel Miles and his Union garrison. None of the three Confederate columns approaching Harpers Ferry had seized its assigned mountain nor even arrived within four miles of its designated target. The September 12 deadline imposed by Special Orders No. 191 had come and passed, and the army still remained badly scattered. In fact, Lee had further divided the part of his army near Boonsboro, sending a portion under Longstreet to Hagerstown to counter a reported advance of Pennsylvania militia from the north. Despite failure to meet his deadlines, Lee seemed unconcerned. McClellan and the Union army lay thirty miles to the east, and the South Mountain range screened the movements of the Confederate columns. Although behind schedule, no reason existed to cancel the mission against Harpers Ferry.

The first Confederates appeared north of Maryland Heights on the afternoon of September 12. These Rebels belonged to Major General Lafayette McLaws, a broad-shouldered Georgian commanding his own division and that of Richard H. Anderson. McLaws grasped the importance of his assignment, noting that so ''long as Maryland Heights was occupied by the enemy, Harper's Ferry could never be occupied by us.''

As McLaws's eight thousand Confederates poured into Pleasant Valley, the general deployed his brigades with three goals in mind: capture Maryland Heights, protect his rear on South Mountain, and prevent a Federal breakout through Pleasant Valley. McLaws gave the crucial task of taking Maryland Heights to the two thousand troops of Joseph B. Kershaw's South Carolina brigade and William Barksdale's Mississippi brigade. The difficult terrain of Maryland Heights presented a formidable challenge to men from the flatlands of South Carolina and Mississippi. Rocky and precipitous mountain slopes defied access to the narrow crest, and brambles and tangled undergrowth hindered visibility, formation, and speed. A road into Solomon's Gap permitted an easy Confederate ascent to the top of Elk Ridge, but once there the Rebels had to trudge through four miles of wilderness. Each step became a triumph. A frustrated Kershaw declared that on September 12 ''the natural obstacles were so great that we only reached a position about a mile from the [end] of the mountain at 6 p.m.'' There, as darkness settled in, the weary Southerners encountered their biggest obstacle in the form of abatis and breastworks defended by Federal infantry.

Colonel Thomas H. Ford of the 32nd Ohio Infantry commanded the Union brigade posted on Maryland Heights. Miles had given Ford this post because he led one of only two Northern regiments at Harpers Ferry with more than a year of service. Although Ford and the 32nd had witnessed limited action in the war, Miles expected them to ''stand the heat'' on Maryland Heights. Ford complained more than once to Miles that the defenses on the mountain were inadequate. ''I made strict examination of the situation,'' Ford later reported, ''and found that no fortifications had been made so as to enable us to resist a superior force.'' Ford suggested several measures to correct these deficiencies. First, he told Miles that Solomon's Gap, four miles north of Maryland Heights on Elk Ridge, was the key to defending the mountain. A battery in the gap

Major General Lafayette McLaws

would ''repel almost any force.'' When Miles vetoed this mode of defense, Ford next requested that a section of artillery be placed at a high point on Maryland Heights known as the ''Lookout.'' Miles objected to this idea as well, informing Ford that it seemed the Ohio colonel wanted ''all of the artillery at Harper's Ferry on Maryland Heights.''

Foiled in his efforts to plant artillery on the crest, Ford ordered huge boulders rolled into the road at Solomon's Gap and requested axes so his infantry could cut fields of fire. Though only a dozen axes were forthcoming, Ford's men cleared a one-hundred-yard perimeter north of the Naval Battery; on the crest, they felled two lines of abatis, behind which they constructed breastworks of log and stone. During their advance on September 12, Kershaw's Confederates encountered these Northern defenses. The opposing forces slept on their arms that night, "within speaking distance. . .and certainly not more than 100 yards apart" along the crest of Maryland Heights. As Colonel Ford wrote, it "was apparent to all that on the morning of the 13th the decisive battle would be fought."

About 6:30 a.m. on the thirteenth, fighting "commenced with great fury" when Kershaw opened his attack. The South Carolinians flushed the Federals back to their breastworks within about twenty minutes, but there the Confederates met "a most obstinate and determined resistance." Two attempts to flank the Union left failed amid hissing lead and snapping tree limbs in the bloody forest of Maryland Heights. Thwarted in his assaults and admitting that "our loss was heavy," Kershaw directed Barksdale to move his brigade down the east face of the mountain to gain the Federal right and rear. Before Barksdale had carried out these orders, the Union line became strangely silent—the Yankees had abandoned their breastworks!

Why had the defenders evacuated their strong position? One bullet gives a clue to the sudden withdrawal. Holding the center and left of the Union position was the 126th New York Infantry. Although a rookie regiment mustered just three weeks earlier, the 126th held its part of the line for more than four hours against Kershaw's persistent veterans. About 11:00 a.m., Colonel Eliakim Sherrill, the regimental commander, was shouting encouragement to his men when a minié ball ripped through his jaw. According to some witnesses, Sherrill's wounding produced panic in the ranks of the 126th; others remembered that confusion spread throughout the entire Federal line when the colonel was shot, prompting Major S. M. Hewitt of the 32nd Ohio to order a general retreat. Whatever the reason, the Northerners abandoned their breastworks and fell back four hundred yards southward to form another line along the crest. This was the situation on the mountain late in the morning of September 13 when Dixon Miles arrived at Thomas Ford's headquarters.

Miles did not like what he saw. While ascending the road leading to Ford's command post, Miles and his staff encountered two companies of the 126th New York retreating toward Harpers Ferry. "Boys, what are you doing here?" inquired a startled and perplexed Miles. "We have been ordered to fall back," responded a New Yorker. "By whom?" demanded Miles. "By some major," explained a soldier. Stunned and infuriated, Miles barked: "There has been no order to give orders to fall back. I have given no order to fall back, and no major could get one unless he got it from me." Miles summoned an aide to guide the companies back to the front, then proceeded to Ford's headquarters, located on the southwest slope of the mountain near the Naval Battery. There he witnessed dozens of stragglers from the 126th moping about in utter confusion.

Presently Miles saw Ford, astride a rearing mount, cursing the men and threatening to shoot them if they refused to go back to the crest. Miles jumped into the fray, darting around and swearing as if on a cattle roundup. The two officers finally ordered a nearby company of infantry to fix bayonets and drive the stragglers up the mountainside. Out of breath, the colonels withdrew to Ford's log cabin headquarters for a consultation. "I cannot hold on," declared a shaken Ford. "You *can* and you *must*," Miles shot back. The meeting continued a bit longer, after which Miles prepared to return to Harpers Ferry. Before he left, the senior colonel apparently hedged on his emphatic instructions to hold Maryland Heights at all costs. Miles acknowledged to Ford that retreat might become necessary, and if so that Ford must spike the heavy guns at the Naval Battery to prevent the enemy's turning them against Federals at the Ferry. These last instructions soon would produce disaster for the Union garrison.

Miles reached the south side of the Potomac just after noon to discover Confederate infantry crowning the crest of Loudoun Heights and massing behind School House Ridge, some one thousand yards west of Bolivar Heights. Major General John G. Walker's division, numbering about two thousand men, had climbed Loudoun Heights without firing a shot, and Stonewall Jackson's column of fourteen thousand—comprising the divisions of J. R. Jones, A. R. Lawton, and A. P. Hill—occupied School House Ridge after completing a fifty-one-mile orbital trek through western Maryland and the panhandle of the Shenandoah Valley.

Despite the Rebel encirclement, Miles still held the high ground at Maryland Heights, and every soldier at Harpers Ferry—from recently recruited privates to Brigadier General Julius White (a lawyer and political appointee who had arrived on the twelfth with his twenty-five-hundred-man brigade and had waived his command to Miles)—knew that so long as Maryland Heights remained in Union hands, the garrison would be secure.

About 3:00 p.m. the unthinkable happened. The troops along the crest of Maryland Heights, who had regrouped after the retreat from the breastworks and faced no further Confederate advance, received peremptory instructions from Colonel Ford: "You are hereby ordered to fall back to Harper's Ferry in good order. *Be careful to do so in good order.*" Dumbfounded by Ford's dictum, the commander on the crest, Lieutenant Colonel S. W. Downey of the 3rd Maryland Potomac Home Brigade, hesitated to obey it. But fifteen minutes after arrival of the first order, Downey's adjutant brought a second identical order to his vacillating chief. "I always have been very careful about obeying orders," Downey sadly reported, and about 3:30 p.m. the Federals commenced withdrawing from Maryland Heights.

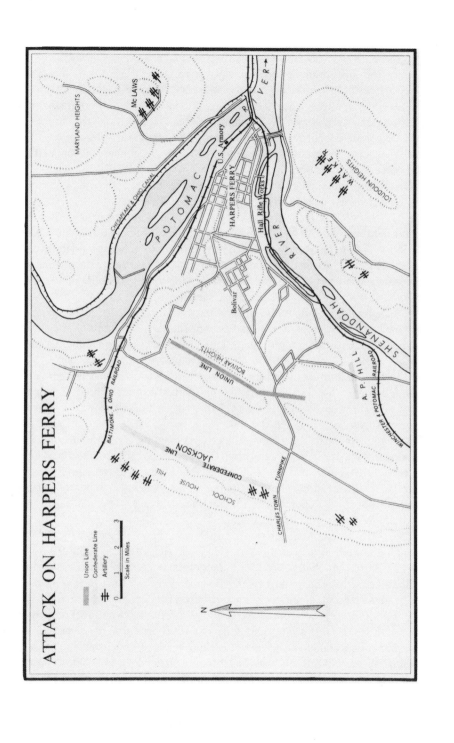

ATTACK ON HARPERS FERRY

Union Line
Confederate Line
Artillery

0   1   2   3
Scale in Miles

N

MARYLAND HEIGHTS

Mc LAWS

POTOMAC RIVER

CHESAPEAKE & OHIO CANAL

U.S. Armory

HARPERS FERRY

Hall Rifle Works

LOUDOUN HEIGHTS

WALKER

Bolivar

SHENANDOAH RIVER

BOLIVAR HEIGHTS

UNION LINE

A. P. HILL

WINCHESTER & POTOMAC RAILROAD

BALTIMORE & OHIO RAILROAD

CONFEDERATE LINE

JACKSON

SCHOOL HOUSE HILL

CHARLES TOWN TURNPIKE

"God almighty!" screamed Dixon Miles, wheeling his horse toward the Federal retreat from his command post on Bolivar Heights. "What does that mean? They are coming down! Hell and damnation! They are coming down!" Union morale crashed as the soldiers in Harpers Ferry watched their comrades snake their way down the slopes of Maryland Heights. "It looks rather hard for us," an Ohio private scribbled tersely in his diary. One Southern writer agreed: "Like a wolf in some cavern of the mountains, [Miles] was about to be smoked out, and forced either to surrender or die defending himself."

Dixon Miles intended no surrender. He knew that Confederate infantry on the mountaintops could cause little harm. If the Federals held on for just a few days—while Confederate artillery got into position to spring the trap door— help might arrive from McClellan's army. Miles summoned Captain Charles H. Russell of the 1st Maryland Cavalry to his headquarters early on the evening of September 13. Russell had operated in western Maryland since June 1862 and knew the territory intimately. Deferring to Russell's knowledge of the region, Miles asked if there was a practical passage through the enemy's lines. When Russell agreed to ride out with a small force of cavalry, Miles ordered the captain to "try to reach somebody that had ever heard of the United States Army, or anybody that knew anything about the United States Army, and report the condition of Harper's Ferry." Assuming that McClellan had reached Frederick, Miles told Russell to aim for that point and report to McClellan that Harpers Ferry had subsistence for forty-eight hours and that Miles could hold out for that long. "If not relieved in that time," Miles urged Russell to warn, "[I] will have to surrender the place."

Russell memorized the message, selected nine of his best troopers, and soon disappeared into the darkness. By dawn of Sunday, September 14, the Marylanders had reached Union lines; by 9:00 a.m., Russell had convened a conference with General McClellan. But McClellan already knew the Rebel movements, their positions, and Robert E. Lee's intentions. George B. McClellan had Special Orders No. 191 in his hands.

Fate had enlisted on the Union side on the afternoon of September 13. While lounging around a bivouac field outside Frederick, Sergeant John Bloss and Private Barton Mitchell of the 27th Indiana Infantry had spied a piece of paper rolled around three unsmoked cigars. Tantalized by their find, the two Hoosiers grabbed the cigars and noticed some writing on the paper. They scanned a page that told of every movement of the Army of Northern Virginia. Bloss and his superiors decided this was no hoax and passed the paper upward to headquarters, where an officer authenticated the handwriting before an understandably skeptical McClellan. A miracle of sorts had brought Special Orders No. 191 to the Federals—not only a miracle of discovery, but a miracle of process that led the crumpled paper to George McClellan's eyes.

Yet discovery of Special Orders No. 191 should have been *insignificant*. The order called for the Harpers Ferry operation to end by September 12. McClellan received the order on the thirteenth, one day after Lee had scheduled the reunification of his army. Indeed, the order was outdated, but its execution had not been completed. With the enemy running late and his forces still scattered, McClellan had Lee's strategic plan in his hands and with it the opportunity to destroy the Army of Northern Virginia. "I think Lee has made a gross mistake," an exuberant McClellan wired President Lincoln in the wee hours of September 13. "I have all the plans of the rebels, and will catch them in their own trap. . . ."

In order to trap the Confederates, McClellan had to break through the gaps of South Mountain. A strike at Fox's and Turner's gaps near Boonsboro would cut off the divisions of Longstreet, John Bell Hood, D. R. Jones, D. H. Hill, and probably snare Robert E. Lee himself. More importantly, a drive through Crampton's Gap west of Burkittsville would seal Lafayette McLaws in a hole and raise the siege of Harpers Ferry. As historian Francis W. Palfrey noted twenty years after the campaign, "The case called for the utmost exertion, and the utmost speed. . . . [McClellan] could not lose and might win by speed, and gained nothing and might lose almost everything by delay."

Unfortunately for the North, McClellan did delay. In his first order issued after the discovery of 191 (dated 6:20 p.m. on the thirteenth), McClellan instructed Sixth Corps commander William B. Franklin to secure Crampton's Gap, but not to move until "daybreak in the morning" of the fourteenth. This inexcusable delay cost the Union army critical hours, and time shifted back to the Confederate side as Stonewall Jackson tightened the noose around Harpers Ferry.

Only sporadic gunfire had disturbed the silence at the Ferry during the night of September 13–14. An occasional shell from Union artillery forced Rebels on School House Ridge and Loudoun Heights to duck behind the ridgetops, but this proved a minor disturbance on an otherwise peaceful Sabbath. Since the infantry on both sides was too far apart for skirmishing, the opponents eyed one another as miniature soldiers deployed on the mountains of the Blue Ridge.

Unknown to the Federals, however, Confederates labored on the slopes of Maryland and Loudoun Heights dragging artillery up abandoned mountain roads. By late morning of the fourteenth, General John G. Walker had five rifled pieces on Loudoun's crest; by 2:00 p.m., General McLaws had three 10-pounder Parrotts and one 3-inch Ordnance Rifle in place on Maryland Heights. Jackson also had batteries in line along School House Ridge. Thus, from each side of a triangle, Confederate gunners prepared to send artillery rounds toward an apparently doomed Federal garrison.

But potential help for the defenders loomed to the northeast. Throughout the morning of the fourteenth, a distant rumble of cannon held the attention of the garrison at Harpers Ferry. Was McClellan coming? wondered the Federals. General Walker heard the same rumble from his position on Loudoun Heights and knew something was happening in the Confederate rear along the South

Major General Thomas Jonathan Jackson

Mountain range. He had wanted to commence firing on Harpers Ferry since 10:00 a.m., but Jackson had ordered him to wait. "I do not desire any of the batteries to open until all are ready on both sides of the river," wigwagged Stonewall's signalmen. "I will let you know when to open all your batteries." Three hours passed with no Confederate bombardment. Jackson, former professor of artillery at the Virginia Military Institute, wanted everything to be perfect; ignoring repeated warnings from Walker of a Yankee advance, Jackson waited for every Southern gun to wheel into place.

Frustrated by his superior's deliberate movements and stated belief that the firing at South Mountain represented nothing more "than a cavalry affair," Walker determined to force a showdown. He paraded two of his regiments in full view of Federal batteries on Bolivar Heights, and, as expected, drew their fire. Walker immediately replied with five guns. "I saw two, three, four, half a dozen puffs of smoke burst out," wrote Captain Edward Hastings Ripley of the 9th Vermont Infantry. From his grassy perch on Bolivar Heights, Ripley then witnessed "a crash, then another and another, and columns of dirt and smoke leap[ing] into the air, as though a dozen young volcanoes had burst forth." "In an instant," continued Ripley, "the bivouac turned into the appearance of a disturbed ant-hill. Artillery, infantry, and cavalry were mixed in an absurd and laughable melee, as the panic increased." Captain Samuel Chapman Armstrong of the 125th New York Infantry recorded a similar experience: "Our regiment was napping and lounging around. . .when suddenly. . .a shell came whizzing into our midst—we saw our helplessness; we were at their mercy; to remain was to be slaughtered, so we ran like hounds to get under the cover of a hillside."

Moments after Walker's initial salvo, concussions also shook the earth from Jackson's guns on School House Ridge. Then some white, gracefully rising puffs floated up from Maryland Heights, followed seconds later by shells plummeting toward Bolivar Heights. "We were between [three] fires," wailed Vermont's Ripley, "and there was no shelter that would protect a rabbit."

The Federal eight-gun battery on Camp Hill particularly suffered from the Southern barrage. Located under the nose of Walker's five rifled pieces on Loudoun Heights, the gunners on Camp Hill experienced a deadly fire that disabled their battery in two hours. One Confederate round ignited a caisson on Camp Hill, which erupted into a seventy-foot spire of white smoke— "A magnificent pyrotechnic display," applauded one Rebel. Many Union soldiers refused to expose themselves to the Confederate cannon, and soon thousands huddled in deep ravines crisscrossing Bolivar Heights. Although the Federals had suffered few casualties, their morale dropped quickly. "I tell you, it is dreadful to be a mark for artillery," admitted Samuel Armstrong of the 125th New York, "bad enough for any but especially for raw troops; it demoralizes them—it rouses one's courage to be able to fight in return, but to sit still and calmly be cut in two is too much to ask.''

Not all the defenders crouched in ravines, however, for a number of Federals held their ground around the Naval Battery on Maryland Heights. Colonel Frederick D'Utassy of the 39th New York Infantry, who commanded Miles's 1st Brigade, had requested permission about noon on the fourteenth to reoccupy the heights. "Damn it!" Miles exclaimed, "[Ford's men] have spiked the guns; it is of no use." When Miles galloped away, D'Utassy turned to the commander's aide-de-camp and confidant, Lieutenant Henry Binney, and asked: "Can I dare to risk it on my own account?" Binney replied that he could give no authorization but suggested D'Utassy do as he thought best. The Austrian-born colonel soon had four companies of infantry en route to Maryland Heights. They reached the Naval Battery just before the Southern bombardment commenced, but because the Rebels on the crest of the mountain were nearly one mile away, D'Utassy encountered no opposition at the battery. Instead of holding the position, however, D'Utassy fell back to Harpers Ferry, taking all the gunpowder at the battery and four spiked 12-pounder guns. He received no censure from Colonel Miles for his impromptu operation.

D'Utassy had proved that the Federals might retake Maryland Heights, but Miles showed no interest. The high ground no longer served any useful purpose, explained the colonel, because the big guns at the Naval Battery had been spiked. Besides, orders demanded that Harpers Ferry—not Maryland Heights—be held ''to the last extremity.'' Miles subsequently launched no further effort to reclaim the Maryland high ground.

When D'Utassy's expedition returned to the Ferry, Confederate bombs were pouring down on the garrison. "At first," wrote Lieutenant James H. Clark of the 125th New York Infantry, "their missiles of death fell far short of our camp; but each succeeding shell came nearer and nearer, until the earth was plowed up at our feet, and our tents torn to tatters." The heavens rained iron for five hours that September Sunday, the storm stopping only with darkness. "As far as the eye could reach in the circle, from the Shenandoah to the Potomac," observed Captain Ripley of the 9th Vermont at dusk on September 14, "was the lurid glare of Jackson's camp-fires, close up around us. The darkness of the night, with the protection it brought us, was so grateful we wished we might always be enwrapped in it." Yet the Federals knew dawn would bring another iron storm; and though the red, white, and blue still floated defiantly above the garrison, the question remained—how much longer?

Colonel Benjamin F. Davis of the 8th New York Cavalry did not intend to wait for the answer. He planned a breakout, and at 7:00 p.m. on the fourteenth, the commanders of all the cavalry units discussed the scheme with Miles at his Harpers Ferry headquarters. Davis served as spokesman, expecting Miles to respect his opinion as a fellow officer in the regular army. He first explained that the cavalry "was of no use" in a siege and noted as well that forage had been exhausted. Davis further suggested that if surrender came, the Federal horses "would be as great a prize as the enemy could get." Miles listened patiently. Davis's arguments made sense, he thought, but what routes of escape were available? And what about the infantry and artillery? They likely also would expect permission to leave.

Following much discussion, Miles consented to a plan permitting the cavalry to cross the Potomac River on a pontoon bridge and ride north toward Sharpsburg. Warning that the infantry must not be told lest the news "cause a stampede," Miles issued the order for the breakout. Davis lost no time in organizing the column, which began moving out about 8:30 p.m., Major Henry Cole's battalion of Marylanders leading the way for fifteen hundred tensely quiet bluecoats. No shots were fired, no shouts heard as the column slipped into the darkness. Eight hours later, after galloping a suspenseful, circuitous route and escaping from close encounters with enemy infantry, Davis and his men stumbled upon General Longstreet's reserve ammunition train, promptly captured it, and escorted the booty north across the Mason-Dixon Line. When the seventy-odd Confederate wagons rolled into Greencastle, Pennsylvania, the cavalrymen rightly counted their adventure a brilliant success. Back at Harpers Ferry, Dixon Miles knew nothing of the cavalry's triumph. Surrounded and anxious, he wondered, "Where is McClellan and his army?"

The Union army was in fact very close by. With the "Lost Order" in McClellan's hands, the Army of the Potomac had moved west on Sunday the fourteenth, advancing up South Mountain and hammering the Confederate rear at Fox's, Turner's, and Crampton's gaps. Unexpected all-day Rebel resistance at Fox's and Turner's gaps near Boonsboro had foiled McClellan's plan "to cut the enemy in two and beat him in detail," but overwhelming Federal numbers had compelled Lee to "look squarely at the facts" and retreat from the passes that night. Although the holding action in the gaps had gained time for the investing forces at Harpers Ferry, Lee was deeply skeptical of success—so doubtful that he informed Lafayette McLaws that the "day has gone against us and this army will go by Sharpsburg and cross the river. It is necessary for you to abandon your position tonight." But McLaws could not execute Lee's order because he was now trapped in Pleasant Valley. South Mountain and Elk Ridge boxed him in from east and west, and Federals at Crampton's Gap and Harpers Ferry nailed the box closed from north and south. Only mistakes committed by the Yankees at Crampton's Gap allowed McLaws additional time to snatch the prize at Harpers Ferry.

At 6:20 p.m. on the thirteenth, McClellan had ordered Sixth Corps chief William B. Franklin to "cut off, destroy, or capture McLaws' command and relieve Colonel Miles." That same order instructed Franklin not to move until daybreak on the fourteenth, thereby wasting eleven precious hours. Franklin marched his twelve thousand men toward Crampton's Gap at dawn, consuming

Major General William Buel Franklin

six hours to traverse just eleven miles on good, dry roads and pausing to wait for reinforcements that never arrived. Noon approached before Franklin neared Burkittsville at the eastern base of Crampton's Gap. Three more hours passed as the Federal commander deployed for an attack against a stone wall defended by a mixed force of five hundred Rebel infantry and dismounted cavalry. One Confederate onlooker mused that the extraordinary caution of the Federals reminded him "of a lion, making exceedingly careful preparations to spring on a plucky little mouse." When the Sixth Corps did spring, it required little time to sweep aside the Rebels at the stone wall. A wave of Union soldiers then began ascending toward Crampton's Gap, each step taking them closer to the rear of Lafayette McLaws and his eight thousand Confederates in Pleasant Valley.

McLaws at first felt only minor concern about the Federals to the north. From Maryland Heights, where he happily directed artillery fire toward Harpers Ferry, he heard cannonading and saw smoke in the area of Crampton's Gap, but General J. E. B. Stuart, who had joined McLaws on the heights, shrugged off the affair as involving only "a brigade of the enemy." Unconvinced by Stuart's certitude, McLaws directed reinforcements toward the gap. Presently the firing grew louder and the smoke much thicker, prompting both generals to ride to Crampton's Gap. Pandemonium greeted the pair at their destination. "We witnessed a scene of the most mortifying panic and confusion," stated Heros von Borcke of Stuart's staff. "Hundreds of soldiers, many of them wounded, were arriving in disorderly array from the fight, while guns and caissons, huddled together with wagons and ambulances, blocked the road." Suddenly, out of the human morass, Brigadier General Howell Cobb came forward screaming: "Dismount, gentlemen, dismount, if your lives are dear to you! The enemy is within fifty yards of us; I am expecting their attack every moment. Oh, my dear Stuart, that I should live to experience such a disaster! What can be done? What can save us?"

Federals swarmed all over the gap. McLaws ordered a withdrawal, but not before the Union attackers took four hundred prisoners from seventeen different Confederate units, as well as seven hundred muskets, one piece of artillery, and three stand of colors—the largest cumulative loss by capture for the Army of Northern Virginia to that time.

Securing the gap had accomplished only one of Franklin's assignments. He had cut off McLaws, but he had neither destroyed him nor relieved Colonel Miles. Pursuit of the disorganized Confederates into Pleasant Valley was Franklin's next move. Instead of pressing ahead with the "utmost activity that a general can exercise," as McClellan had instructed, Franklin halted at the top of the gap to reorganize his command. This proved a costly mistake that granted additional time to the embattled Confederates. "Fortunately," wrote McLaws, "night came on and allowed a new arrangement of the troops. . .to meet the changed aspect of affairs." McLaws gathered his scattered forces in Pleasant Valley that night, withdrew Southern infantry from Maryland Heights, and deployed his eight thousand men in two lines across the floor of the valley. "My offer of Battle was intended as a bluff," the Georgian admitted years after the war—a bluff that succeeded admirably.

Sunrise on September 15 revealed McLaws's new position to Franklin, who concluded that "it would be suicidal to attack it." As if a clone of McClellan himself, the Sixth Corps commander dispatched a courier to relate to Little Mac the absurdity that the "enemy outnumber me two to one. I fear I cannot advance without reinforcements." The force sent to rescue Harpers Ferry thus halted because of Franklin's self-delusion, halted just six miles from Dixon Miles and the besieged Federals who had nervously watched for signs of Confederate activity through the long night of September 14.

Stonewall Jackson had realized that artillery alone would not subdue the garrison. Late on the afternoon of the fourteenth he ordered A. P. Hill's division "to move along the left bank of the Shenandoah, and thus turn the enemy's left flank" on Bolivar Heights. Marching his six brigades obliquely to the right behind School House Ridge, Hill reached the Shenandoah and slowly made his way along its bank. He soon spied "an eminence crowning the extreme left of the enemy's line, bare of all earthwork, the only obstacles being abatis of fallen timber." This eminence became Hill's primary target.

During the night of the fourteenth, Hill's men struggled up steep ravines and through tangled abatis to reach the rear of the Federal line along Bolivar Heights. The Yankees on the left heard the commotion and frequently fired into the darkness. "We were told that a battle was expected here every minute," recalled Captain Armstrong of the 125th New York Infantry. "We stood in the cool and thoughtful evening hour after hour, some of us awaiting, as it seemed, our final summons." Yet no battle erupted, much to the relief of a South Carolinian in Maxcy Gregg's Confederate brigade: "Why we were allowed to climb the precipitous height I never could understand," exclaimed J. F. J. Caldwell. "A handful of the enemy could have beaten back an army here, for it was so steep that a man could hardly carry his arms up it. And they had night to assist them also." With the Federals offering virtually no resistance, Hill positioned two brigades within 150 yards of a redoubt on the Union left. The remaining four brigades and five batteries of artillery rested comfortably a thousand yards *behind* the Federal flank. Hill's three thousand men and twenty-three guns anticipated daylight, and Hill confidently predicted that "the fate of Harper's Ferry was sealed."

Jackson also ordered additional firepower closer to the left of Bolivar Heights to support Hill's brigades. On the night of the fourteenth and morning of the fifteenth, Stapleton Crutchfield, Jackson's chief of artillery, moved ten guns from School House Ridge across the Shenandoah River to a shelf at the base of Loudoun Heights. Crutchfield's cannoneers could enfilade Bolivar Heights and render unsafe the ravines in which so many Federals had sought shelter. Because Jackson's movements had been shrouded by darkness, no one at Harpers Ferry knew the extent of the new Confederate alignment. The Federals did sense that Rebels were breathing much closer, and Louis B. Hull of the 60th Ohio Infantry observed a "general feeling of depression" among the defenders, who seemed "to think that we will have to surrender or be cut to pieces."

Dense fog blanketed the area around Harpers Ferry at dawn on Monday, September 15. When the misty curtain began to rise that morning, the scene revealed Confederate cannon at every corner of the stage. Bright lights of orange and yellow soon flashed across the hillsides, followed in seconds by thundering reports and whistling shells. "The *infernal screech owls* came hissing and singing," stated a frightened Lieutenant James Clark of the 115th New York Infantry, "then bursting, plowing great holes in the earth, filling our eyes with dust, and tearing many giant trees to atoms." A reporter for the *New York Times* showed similar trepidation: "Their batteries were so arranged as to enfilade us completely. To hold out longer seemed madness."

An hour of ferocious bombardment illuminated several facts for Dixon Miles: his men had no cover; his batteries had no long-range ammunition; his flank had been turned; and no relief from the Army of the Potomac was in sight. In addition, Rebel infantry stood poised to strike his left, and amid a barrage that pounded every foot of Bolivar Heights it was impossible to organize an effective defense. Miles turned his thought to surrender, convening a council-of-war with two of his brigade commanders and General Julius White. In the "midst of shell and round shot," and after some acrimonious discussion, the group decided unanimously to capitulate. Between 8:00 and 9:00 a.m., white flags and kerchiefs began bobbing along Bolivar Heights.

Lingering fog and dense smoke masked these symbols of surrender from some Confederate batteries, which continued to direct fire against the Union lines. One Rebel missile found an improbable target in Federal commander Miles. As the despondent colonel traveled across the heights just after the surrender, an ungracious shell exploded behind him, nearly cutting away his legs and inflicting a mortal wound. With Miles out of action, General White rode toward School House Ridge to seek terms from Stonewall Jackson. Jackson demanded unconditional surrender; White formally capitulated; and Jackson ordered A. P. Hill to arrange specific details. Stonewall then sent a courier to Sharpsburg with welcome news for General Lee: "Through God's blessing, Harper's Ferry and its garrison are to be surrendered."

Three days behind schedule, the Confederates had taken their prize at last. And what a prize! Harpers Ferry yielded 73 pieces of artillery, 13,000 small arms, 200 wagons, and 12,500 prisoners—the largest surrender of United States troops during the Civil War.

Jackson and his veterans had little time to savor their victory. Lee desperately needed help along the banks of Antietam Creek. Jackson must march north immediately. Most of his soldiers departed Harpers Ferry by the evening of September 16, the bulk of them with full stomachs and many with new clothes and shoes. A. P. Hill stayed behind with his division to gain some rest and parole the Union prisoners. On September 17, two days after the surrender at Harpers Ferry, Lee and McClellan clashed at Antietam in an unimaginably bloody contest. When Union casualties at Antietam are combined with the garrison surrendered at Harpers Ferry, the Federals lost in two days more than twenty-five thousand men. No other two-day period during the war brought such a heavy cost to the Northern war effort.

Although Antietam has overshadowed both Harpers Ferry and South Mountain, Harpers Ferry remained on the front pages of newspapers for seven weeks after the surrender. The government, the press, and the army all demanded answers and scapegoats for the debacle. The War Department organized a special commission to investigate the matter; under the chairmanship of Major General David Hunter, this commission interviewed forty-four witnesses and asked eighteen hundred questions during fifteen days of testimony. Queries focused on the competence and loyalty of Colonel Miles, his execution of the defense, the actions of his subordinates, opportunities for escape, and opportunities to rescue the garrison.

Testimony produced more than nine hundred pages of evidence, and the commission's findings labeled Colonel Thomas H. Ford the primary scapegoat. The official report declared that Ford conducted the defense of Maryland Heights "without ability, and [he] abandoned his position without sufficient cause, and [he] has shown throughout such a lack of military capacity as to disqualify him. . . for a command in the service." The commission also censured General McClellan for failing to relieve and protect Harpers Ferry, and, despite "extreme reluctance" to discuss the deceased Miles ("an officer who cannot appear before any earthly tribunal"), spoke of Miles's "incapacity, amounting to almost imbecility [for] the shameful surrender of this important post." "Had the garrison been slower to surrender or the Army of the Potomac swifter to march," the commission reasoned, "the enemy would have been forced to raise the siege or have been taken in detail."

A Northern private at Harpers Ferry, after seeing Stonewall Jackson ride through the surrendered Federal ranks on Bolivar Heights, had a simpler explanation: "Boys, he ain't much for looks, but if we'd had him on our side, we wouldn't have been caught in this trap." That may well have been true, but the private's assessment overlooked the larger truth that Robert E. Lee enjoyed remarkably good luck in his gamble at Harpers Ferry. Insisting on an unreasonable timetable and willing to divide his badly outnumbered army on the basis of *his* reading of George B. McClellan, Lee had courted catastrophe at the picturesque Ferry where two fabled rivers join their waters.

R O B E R T   K .   K R I C K

The Army of Northern Virginia in September 1862

Its Circumstances, Its Opportunities, and Why It Should Not Have Been at Sharpsburg

During the first days of September in 1862, the Army of Northern Virginia rode the crest of a military tide of remarkable proportions. Nine weeks earlier the Confederate capital at Richmond had perched apparently at the mercy of a mighty Federal army that swarmed around its outerworks. Now the Confederates who had been bottled up in the shadow of Richmond's spires were surging toward the outskirts of Washington.

The metamorphosis sprang from the advent of R. E. Lee as commander of the Army of Northern Virginia. His was the first sure hand at the controls of a major component of the military picture in the Virginia theater. Firmly, calmly, and steadily Lee had imposed order on what had been Confederate chaos, and simultaneously spread disorder in the enemy camp.

After driving McClellan from the gates of Richmond, Lee had reoriented the war northward to the plains of Manassas. The Second Battle of Manassas (or Bull Run, as Northerners were wont to call it) had cost the South relatively little blood, by the ghastly standards then in operation, but it had required a great deal of toil and sweat. Richard H. Anderson's division reached the battlefield only tardily, and neither Lafayette McLaws nor D. H. Hill reached the field in time to participate at all. The army fought brilliantly in the exhausting heat, while its leaders cooperated in tactical initiatives of almost fabulous proportions.

The shining Confederate successes of late August reached fruition despite the fact that almost no rations filtered through the moribund Southern commissary system to the men on the front lines. Two of the more familiar mots attributed to Napoleon Bonaparte succinctly define the quintessential role of the commissariat, which at first blush seems no more than a quasi-military staff detail. "Biscuits make war possible," the emperor said, and again: "An army marches on its stomach." The Confederates who made Second Manassas a dazzling Southern high point despite marching without biscuits, on empty stomachs, achieved what they did in line with yet another Napoleonic dictim: ''In war the moral is to the material as three to one.'' As August turned into September, Confederate leaders might have wondered if the operative question just then was if there was anything at all the army of Northern Virginia could *not* do, and biscuits be damned?

At the same time the quartermaster and ordnance functions of Lee's army had unraveled to an alarming extent. The logistical chaos inherent almost as certain in rapid advances and victories as well as in rapid retreats and defeats overwhelmed those departments. Individuals achieved some logistical miracles by dint of lavish energy (it is impossible, for instance, to imagine E. P. Alexander— then the army's chief ordnance officer—failing to accomplish at least his highest-priority goals); but the Army of Northern Virginia had outstripped its support services long before its renewed advance placed the broad Potomac River athwart the line of supply. The lush harvest of captured Northern ordnance reaped on the plains of Manassas, for example, lay unsecured long after the armies had moved away, and some of it fell prey to Federals roaming over country long since abandoned by any major Southern force. It would be difficult to over-emphasize the casual approach of Civil War armies, particularly Southern ones, to staff functions of all sorts.

The monumental inadequacy of commissary, quartermaster, and ordnance services left Lee with tremendous problems, but they did not create a situation in which he seriously considered any alternative other than further advance. Some students of the war in the East argue that Lee should not have attempted a Maryland venture at all. He did not win the war there; accordingly, the war could not have been won there; or else it could have, and Lee was not up to the test. Specious syllogisms of that stripe have been applied to almost every other of the army's campaigns.

In fact, the vagaries and anomalies that bedevil human endeavor continually posed corollary problems. Random bounces and angles always affect human equations, whether hitting a baseball through the grass clumps, cinders, and human obstacles of a drawn-in infield, or moving tens of thousands of men through narrow roads in quest of a military advantage. The progress of Lee's advance into Maryland turned to a degree on one of the most famous small bounces of the war, the familiar business of three cigars and Special Orders No. 191. It also caromed off other apparently minuscule mistakes and coincidences that we can identify—for instance, the erroneous report of Federal forces at Chambersburg that led to a casual-turned-crucial adjustment in troop dispositions.

Lee's decision to move into Maryland cannot be rationally gainsaid. He stood at the cutting edge of a revolutionary movement. A year and more of Confederate failure, some of it abject in scope, had turned into a flood tide of success that he must exploit in hopes that it would lead to the sort of victory that might assure his country's independence. The difficulties that his shrunken army faced could not deter him from grasping the moment. Ten days later, when fate had denied Lee and his army the circumstances he had sought, he fought the battle of Sharpsburg, or Antietam. That fight he should not have made. The effort to find the right set of circumstances, however, he had to make.

Ample and numerous military and political reasons for a move across the Potomac appealed to Lee as he contemplated the prospect. Three of them deserve at least brief dilation in this context: the depleted countryside south of the Potomac badly needed surcease; Maryland offered Lee chance for maneuver, which he did incomparably well, and for high-stake fruits as the result of any victory he could attain; and, Maryland seemed politically ripe for liberation from what looked like an intolerable Federal yoke.

The effect of warfare on both countryside and civilians had shocked innocent Southerners who went to war in a frolicsome mood. Career officers who had served in Mexico, or otherwise had been exposed to the indecency that is war, knew what to expect, but others did not. For several months in 1862 the entire state of Virginia north of the James River lay open to Federal occupation, a situation not to be repeated until much later, during the war's final phase. Lee sought to divert the war from his native state not just for humanitarian reasons but for military ones. If he was to subsist his army in Virginia again soon—and obviously he had no intention of remaining north of the Potomac permanently— it was necessary to give the Old Dominion a chance to recuperate and replenish.

R. E. Lee's knack for maneuver had not yet blazed on enough fields to ensure his lasting fame, but he himself must have known that his great skill in that line demanded the best possible forum, especially since his vastly outnumbered nation offered little opportunity to operate on a grander scale. The verities of military geography in Virginia, which are ignored to an alarming degree in historical studies of the war, made Northern Virginia a poor stage upon which to strut. Maryland's narrow breadth offered little better prospect, to be sure, but Lee did not necessarily limit his trans-Potomac horizon to that state. Furthermore, the inalterable Federal ground rules about protecting Washington served to straiten enemy military options and broaden Lee's. Finally, a victory north of the Potomac offered alluring visions of prizes to be won that made anything attainable south of the river look small by comparison.

There can be no question that Lee and the important Southern leaders believed that by moving the Army of Northern Virginia into Maryland they would be carrying succor to a friendly state. In April 1861 the citizens of Baltimore had stoned and killed some Massachusetts soldiers marching through the town. Lincoln had in essence suspended the Constitution, jailed uncooperative elected leaders, and generally pinned Maryland to the Union with bayonets. Young men from eastern Maryland crossed the Potomac to the number of at least twenty thousand and turned themselves into stalwart soldiers for the Confederacy. James Ryder Randall's immensely popular Confederate war song, ''Maryland, My

Maryland,'' seemed to reflect the state's travail with its opening line: ''The despot's heel is on thy soil. . . .''

Lee was to learn that the fiery Southern sympathies of eastern Maryland did not extend to the western panhandle. The largely German populace there felt far more empathy northward to their kinfolk and economic peers in Pennsylvania than southward across the wide river. What Virginians viewed as outrages against law and decency in the suppression of Maryland political processes mattered little if at all in Keedysville and Frederick. Furthermore, the administration's iron hand in eastern Maryland had succeeded in suppressing the dissent. A year and a half of war also had rubbed much of the glitter from perceptions of its nature. Even had his path led him to the longitude of Baltimore, Lee would have found only vestiges of the uprising en masse that would have greeted such an occasion one year earlier.

For these and other reasons the army crossed the Potomac on September 4–7 and went into camp near the town of Frederick. Most of the men who traversed the fords near Leesburg sang Randall's famous song during their passage. Dozens of picturesque quotes bring that scene alive for us today. One of Stonewall Jackson's staff officers, for instance, described the picture as the 10th Virginia Infantry, preceded by its band, waded through the ford with the general beside them on a ''cream-colored. . .horse. . . .amid shouts of the soldiers.'' ''It was a noble spectacle,'' the eyewitness told his diary, ''the broad river, fringed by the lofty trees in full foliage; the exuberant wealth of the autumnal wild flowers down to the very margin of the stream and a bright green island stretched away to the right.'' The underfed, and even unfed, men in the ranks probably appreciated the setting less than they did the canal boat full of ''noble'' melons that fell into their hands on the north bank of the river.

The misapprehension of the Confederate high command about Maryland's enthusiasm for things Southern doubtless was abetted by the reception Lee and Jackson received personally. The two men were certifiable celebrities and attracted eager attention everywhere they went, even in western Maryland. A young Englishman described the Marylanders who flocked around Lee as he rode out of the water on his next visit to these parts as ''patriotic ladies with small feet and big umbrellas,'' led by a woman ''with a face like a door-knocker. . . .'' These earnest folks tried to place ''an enormous wreath'' around the neck of Lee's horse, which reasonably enough refused to cooperate. Given the traditional English understatement, the scene must have been memorable indeed. But women bearing wreaths did nothing to augment the infantry count.

The generals over whom the civilians made such a fuss happened to be hurting to one degree or another as a result of a succession of three peculiar but unrelated injuries. Lee had suffered badly wrenched hands on August 31 when his horse shied abruptly and twisted the loosely held reins in the general's grasp. On September 6, Stonewall Jackson mounted a ''strong-sinewed, powerful'' horse presented by an admiring Marylander in order to try out the gift. The animal, unimpressed by the honor, reared and fell over backward on her rider, leaving Mighty Stonewall stunned and in pain for at least a day. James Longstreet's travail had pedestrian rather than equestrian roots. A boot-chafed heel refused to mend, leaving Lee's highest-ranking subordinate obliged to wear a "wobbly carpet slipper" during the army's sojourn in Maryland. There is no evidence that any of these physical woes bore directly on the military situation, but they are worth bearing in mind when contemplating the state of the Army of Northern Virginia.

Confederate strength at Sharpsburg was pitifully small. Arguments raged through the postwar years about precise numbers and losses at Sharpsburg (and elsewhere), and the publication of those arguments grew into a virtual cottage industry both North and South. Without wading into that sticky morass more than shoetop deep it is safe to certify that even at day's end on September 17 Lee had not put forty thousand men on the field. The number in fact probably was a good deal fewer than that, and may have been not much more than thirty thousand. To avoid quibbling, let it be stipulated that Lee had far fewer men at Sharpsburg than on any other of his major fields—perhaps only half as many. That salient verity hangs over every discussion of the events of September 1862.

The shortage of manpower in the ranks must dominate our consideration of Lee's circumstances. Other factors, however, deserve at least passing mention. The "artillery hell" at Sharpsburg, to use S. D. Lee's phrase, was a brew concocted of 6-pounder guns clobbered by Napoleons and 3-inch rifles and even 20-pounder Parrotts. No fewer than 125 Confederate guns were of painfully short-ranged and virtually obsolete varieties. Lee dissolved quite a number of his under-gunned artillery batteries within weeks after Sharpsburg. Confederate cavalrymen, on the other hand, still stood almost impossibly tall in the saddle relative to their less adroit foemen. On a far more subjective level there lurked the matter of geographical stimulus. One Virginia artillerist grumped drolly: "I believe that the confounded Yankees can shoot better in the United States than they can when they come to Dixieland."

The striking shortage of men in Lee's army during its chapter north of the river requires careful explanation. That a rapid movement of an army into enemy country should leave stragglers in its wake is axiomatic. The staggering diminution of the Army of Northern Virginia during the two weeks under discussion here, however, not only was unprecedented for that army but also never was to be repeated. Ten months later the same army moved across the same ground in a campaign that went much farther north before turning back from Gettysburg. The army obviously labored in that campaign under the same geographical vicissitudes, multiplied by degree, and under other disadvantages as well. What factors operated to make the Maryland campaign a straggling nightmare for Lee?

One factor unique for its scope in September 1862 was the matter of shoes.

Major General James Longstreet

Confederates suffered for want of adequate footgear throughout the war: they marched barefoot through the snow to reach Fredericksburg later in 1862; they left bloody footprints on ice, reminiscent of Valley Forge, during the bad winter of 1863–64 in East Tennessee; some preliminary movements at Gettysburg were more oriented to finding shoes than to tactics; and in July 1864 Jubal Early put a temporary bridle on his raid to Washington, D.C., coincidentally while not far from Sharpsburg, Maryland, in order to wait for shoes. Never was the problem more pervasive, however, and never did it have so great an operational impact on the Army of Northern Virginia, as it did in September 1862.

This setting does not offer adequate space to prove the point with definition, but several samples by way of illustration will illuminate the matter. A Virginia infantryman recounted his struggle: "My shoes had begun to give out, and I had to fasten the soles to the upper leathers by making holes through each and tying them together with leather shoe-strings passed through these holes, a device that did not serve to prevent gravel and sand from freely entering the shoes to my great discomfort, impeding my marching and compelling me at times to fall behind the line." Another sufferer who "went through the Maryland campaign bare-footed" cited a concomitant difficulty to sore soles— "Our feet were also sunburned and blistered on top," he complained, "which was equally painful."

The shabbiness that began at his feet made the average Confederate soldier a wonderfully unprepossessing warrior. What seem to be the only extant photographs of the Army of Northern Virginia under arms record this tattered state on the streets of Frederick. One of the tatterdemalions encountered there "a very pretty young woman" wearing Union colors who eyed her recent, if temporary, conqueror and said "in the most contemptuous way, with a sneer on her face . . . 'You *are* a nice specimen, you miserable ragamuffin rebel!' "

For their part, the Southern boys found little to like in the townspeople of western Maryland. A lieutenant from Virginia described the citizens of both Sharpsburg and Keedysville as "the ugliest women and men I ever saw. . . . They looked as if they had been smoked for half a century and then dried. They were chunky and nearly as long one way as the other. I saw but one family that presented at all a symmetrical appearance."

One man slogging patiently in the ranks who was fortunate enough to have a pair of shoes wound up marching barefoot anyway. The heat and dust, he said, made such an unpalatable blend inside his vestigial shoes that he voluntarily took them off and slung them over the end of his rifle. The dust, though hardly a genuine military impediment, added to the misery that laid men out by the dozens and eventually by the thousands on the roadsides. The fine gritty powder "had so completely covered us," wrote a member of the 12th Virginia, "that it was only by the voice that we could recognize one another."

Ugly marching weather exacerbated the discomfort of poorly shod soldiers.

The weather probably does not deserve to be chalked up on the tote board as a separate entry, but at least consider it as an adjunct to the travails of men in the ranks. The twelve-day period preceding the battle of Sharpsburg remained uniformly hot and parched. Contemporary newspapers spoke of 1862's September as the driest in memory. The nearest available weather readings, from down the river at Georgetown, show a 2:00 p.m. temperature of at least seventy-seven degrees for each day between September 5 and 16. The highest reading at that hour was eighty-eight and the average stood above eighty. (Higher temperatures later in the afternoon seem likely, but no readings were made during daylight hours other than at 2:00 p.m.) The mist that hung in the air on September 16 and turned into a steady rain that night must have come as a real boon to dust-choked foot soldiers. By then, however, about one-half of the Southern soldiers enjoying the relief were doing so too far from Sharpsburg to be of any use at all to Lee.

The abject failure of Lee's quartermaster function found a fully equivalent counterpart in the collapse of his commissary system. The hungry men described above during the August campaign and at the river crossing had only just begun to feel the pangs of hunger that awaited them in Maryland. Soldier after soldier, writing at the time without the opportunity for postwar comparisons, referred to the ordeal as "The Green Corn Campaign," or some variant on that refrain. Green corn, unsalted, served poorly as a vegetable and did nothing to substitute for the meat and bread that were nonexistent. Ripe corn cooked in the morning spoiled in haversacks during the day, in the absence of salt. Men too late for the ripe corn settled for corn that was literally green. Digestive tracts rebelled in both instances, leaving more thousands of soldiers littering the roadsides. Even the scavenged corn sometimes was interdicted under Lee's stringent orders protecting private property. Lieutenant William E. Cameron, a postwar mayor of Petersburg and governor of Virginia, attempted to stop some soldiers from carrying corn from a farmer's field, but succumbed to a bribe of a half dozen ears—small and underdeveloped ones at that.

A Union soldier vividly described Confederate dead at Sharpsburg in a manner that referred to their diet. David L. Thompson, whose 9th New York (Hawkins' Zouaves) is memorialized by about the most imposing unit marker on the battlefield today, described the Southern corpses as "undersized men mostly. . .with sallow, hatchet faces, and clad in 'butternut.' " As Thompson "looked down on the poor, pinched faces, worn with marching and scant fare, all enmity died out. There was no 'secession' in those rigid forms. . . ."

The best witness on record about the starving conditions of the Army of Northern Virginia is Mary Bedinger Mitchell. From her convenient vantage point as a civilian in Shepherdstown throughout the entire war, Mary put in context a degree of hunger both absolute and—most important for our purposes—relative to other campaigns:

When I say that they were hungry, I convey no impression of the gaunt starvation that looked from their cavernous eyes. . . . I saw the troops march past us every summer for four years, and I know something of the appearance of a marching army, both Union and Southern. There are always stragglers, of course, but never before *or after* [emphasis added] did I see anything comparable to the demoralized state of the Confederates at this time. Never were want and exhaustion more visibly put before my eyes, and that they could march or fight at all seemed incredible.

The straggling induced by environmental and supply factors posed an apparently insuperable problem. Later campaigns of even greater rigor, however, did not succumb to straggling on this scale. To some degree an improvement in supply services contributed to the better subsequent record. Another factor to consider at the same time is the shortage of officers on hand who had the rank and experience necessary to cope with the difficulty. The shriveled military organizations that fought for Lee at Sharpsburg had lost their cohesiveness. Fifty-man regiments putatively included a ten-company hierarchy plus an establishment of field officers and other regimental headquarters; in fact, fifty men were one-half of the paper strength of a single company. By the close of action on September 17 it was a fortunate brigade that still had so seasoned an officer as a colonel to lead it. One brigade in the famous old division that had been Stonewall Jackson's own ended the day commanded by a captain who was succeeding two other captains already shot down while acting in a position designated for a brigadier general.

A solid one-half of Lee's army, led into Maryland in September 1862 by its ordinary complement of officers, would have met and solved the straggling problem. All of Lee's army units, however, reduced in net numbers to one-half of their normal size, posed an entirely different problem. That command problem simply would not be solved.

To the physical and organizational problems bedeviling the army must be added a tincture of psychological or spiritual malaise. Some men straggled and deserted out of fear, laziness, and lack of commitment; but they did so in all Civil War campaigns—have done so in all military settings throughout recorded history. The implications for these particular soldiers of crossing into Maryland, however, caused many of them honest discomfort unrelated to simple faint-heartedness. A Virginia boy in John G. Walker's brigade, uninitiated into the mysteries of apostrophes but close to the army's pulse, told his diary on September 5: "I dont like the idea, as I dont like to invade anybodys Country." The order to cross the Potomac elicited "a considerable murmur of disappointment," to use its historian's delicate phrase, from a North Carolina regiment also assigned to General Walker. Men from the Old North State apparently suffered pangs of this sort more than most of their peers. Large disaffected areas in the western part of the state doubtless contributed to that atmosphere. Leading politicians and journalists in North Carolina who waxed both noisy and noisome against the Confederate government added impetus to the uneasy feelings of their boys far from home.

All of the factors that added up to straggling of unparalleled severity were magnified by the novelty of the situation. The war by then was a year and a half old. September 1862, however, would witness the crest of the very first full campaign of the Lee-Jackson model of the Army of Northern Virginia. The men and boys strewn across northern Virginia and western Maryland with bare blistered feet, empty stomachs, inadequate leadership, and occasionally queasy consciences, had not known anything like this before. Until a few weeks earlier, Joseph E. Johnston had led their army everywhere it went, and Johnston either did not have lightning advances in his repertoire or—his admirers would say—no one ever gave him the chance to employ one. In either case, the veterans of seventeen months of war found themselves in an entirely new experience.

When like vicissitudes faced the army in the same region the next summer it had evolved into a much sterner utensil. Quartermasters, commissaries, line officers, and psyches all had hardened into an entity recognizable as R. E. Lee's army. The June 1863 movement through the scenes of the September 1862 Maryland campaign left almost no stragglers or deserters in its wake.

A recent statistical analysis of regimental strengths at Sharpsburg yielded these averages per regiment: Union—346; Confederate—166. By contrast, the careful John Bigelow, in his outstanding history of the Chancellorsville campaign, computed regimental strengths in that later struggle as: Union—433; Confederate—409. The eight months between Sharpsburg and Chancellorsville surely should have seen some erosion of unit strength in that era of poorly managed replacement systems. It is appropriate, therefore, to suggest that Confederate unit strength at Sharpsburg languished at levels far lower than half of the norm.

Students of Sharpsburg must adjust their thinking (and continually readjust it, because the focus will slip) to avoid subconsciously evaluating brigade manuevers in the ordinary light. The 8th Virginia Infantry reported thirty-four men in its ranks; the 8th South Carolina reported forty-five; and the 56th Virginia had eighty men under arms. In that context, brigade actions were little more than equivalent to regimental ones both before and after this low point.

Francis W. Palfrey, in his early standard Northern account of the battle, delivered himself of the unctuous partisan pronouncement that Lee invented the straggling story as an ex post facto expedient to explain away his own shortcomings. If that was the case, Lee was devious enough to prepare his excuse well in advance. In a very lengthy and decidedly hortatory general order (No. 102) dated September 4, Lee excoriated stragglers as "useless members of the service . . .especially deserving odium," and promised them "the punishment due to their misconduct.'' He exhorted the steadfast men in the ranks to take steps to hold their more timid comrades to the colors.

Two days after he delivered his army back to the Virginia shore, Lee devoted the majority of a letter (more than five hundred words) to Jefferson Davis to the straggling problem that had ''greatly paralyzed'' him. Although he couched his comments in careful, cultured phrases, Lee boldly suggested application of the death penalty to stragglers. ''It ought to be construed into desertion in face of the enemy,'' the worried general declared, and be accordingly subject to ''the most summary punishment. . . .'' Lee's poise and genteel demeanor make so stark a pronouncement seem harsh and unbalanced at first glance. When Stonewall Jackson rasped suggestions about shooting stragglers, or bayonetting them, contemporaries recorded the fact with almost wry amusement: the humorless old Calvinistic rascal was just being ornery again. Lee's entirely serious refrain in the same vein should jolt to attention anyone uncertain about the seriousness of the question. It is published in the primary volume of the *Official Records* for the Maryland campaign. Examples of strength statistics that Lee supplied to Davis cited two adjacent brigades on his right center that numbered 120 and 100 men.

To carry the straggling and desertion strain to its larger, warwide conclusion, is to open a question too little discussed and but rarely understood. R. E. Lee solved his straggling problem for all practical purposes soon after Sharpsburg. The degree of chronic straggling endemic to any army in the field always continued, of course, but at a tolerable level. When Lee made the army his own, and bent its staff functions to his own purposes, acute straggling disappeared.

Desertion, however, gradually grew to proportions that most students of the Confederacy simply have not imagined. As suggested above, North Carolina troops suffered disproportionately from the malady. During the spring after Sharpsburg, Lee bewailed the ''frequent desertions from the North Carolina regiments. . . .'' Within the same week Lee received a plaintive plea from talented young General William Dorsey Pender—himself a brightly distinguished North Carolinian at the head of a fine brigade from his native state. Pender reported the loss of two hundred men from a single North Carolina regiment within the past thirty days and gloomily told his army commander that he expected that the ''matter will grow from bad to worse.'' In a concurrent letter to his wife, Dorsey Pender sorrowfully wrote, ''Poor old N.C., she will disgrace herself just when the worst is over. . . .''

Revisionist work now afoot intending to lower North Carolina's relative desertion rate will need to use hundreds of thousands of original service records to achieve definition. Meanwhile, the official summary of Confederate deserters compiled by the United States provost marshal general shows that nearly one-half of all Confederate officers who deserted to the enemy came from North

Carolina. The deserting commissioned Carolinians outnumbered the second-place state (Tennessee) by nearly three to one and the third-place state (Virginia) by more than five to one. The same report covering enlisted ranks awards the trophy to North Carolina by a two-to-one margin.

The Federal provost report probably is impeachable to some degree, even if its relative measurements retain validity. The degree of permanent desertion revealed by a conservative scouring of Confederate service records, however, stands beyond contradiction. The 33rd Virginia fought throughout the war as one of five regiments in what probably was the most famous brigade in Southern service, Jackson's own original Stonewall Brigade. No fewer than 354 men—more than one in four who saw service with the unit—deserted permanently from the 33rd Virginia. That staggering number does not include any of the men who went absent without leave for a time; nor any of the men reported as deserters who later returned, nor anyone who just disappeared from the rolls mysteriously, without pejorative comment from the record keepers. Perhaps some of the strayed 354 soldiers found subsequent service with cavalry detachments, both regular and irregular (and not infrequently *highly* irregular), roaming their Shenandoah Valley homeland. None known to have such later affiliation was included in the 354 total, and any inadvertently included surely would be countered by other deserters slipping through the loopholes in the benign set of standards applied to the service records.

Few students of the war would expect a permanent desertion rate anywhere near 25 percent for any Army of Northern Virginia mainline unit, to say nothing of one of the most famous regiments of its old guard. Straggling from the army in Maryland has been extensively discussed in print, but permanent desertion generally has not received much attention. Both the short- and long-term problems deserve exhaustive consideration because they struck at the substance of the army.

To offset in part its difficulties and straggling, the Army of Northern Virginia could look during its Maryland venture to the steady coalescence of a new system of high command. Lee's emerging reliance on two well-organized and distinct corps, ably led by Longstreet and Jackson, was settling into a comfortable habit that had yielded astonishing success at Second Manassas and was well on its way to becoming the army's trademark. The arrangement remained informal for two more months because until November 1862 Confederate law made no provision for corps, nor for general officer rank between major general and full general. Informal though they remained in September, Lee's corps and their commanders operated at a level of tactical control far superior to that achieved by the high-command arrangements of their foe.

Lee's intermediate command also gave promise of moving toward efficiency. The egregious failures of Benjamin Huger, John B. Magruder, and Theophilus H. Holmes during the Seven Days campaign prompted Lee to purge them gently from the army. Problems persisted in some divisional commands, notably those led by interim officers beyond their depth; but overall the Army of Northern Virginia would find far better leadership from general officers in September than it had experienced during June. The realignments included, to generalize, Richard H. Anderson vice Huger, Lafayette McLaws vice Magruder, and John G. Walker vice Holmes. Each of those constituted a substantive upgrading in quality; taken together they held the potential for enormous positive impact. On the other hand, the huge list of officers fighting with the army for the last time, as summarized below, gives vivid testimony to the degree of flux still operating in the command system.

Stonewall Jackson's brother-in-law, Daniel Harvey Hill, was destined to hold center stage longer during the Maryland campaign, and under brighter lights, than any of his fellow division commanders. Neither of the two pivotal scenes starring D. H. Hill showed him to best advantage. The contumacious Hill snarled so regularly and acerbically at the world around him that even Lee, perhaps the least contentious general officer commissioned on either side, complained of his subordinate's "queer temperament" and declared "that he croaked." That last verb has fallen out of ordinary usage, but a random glance at almost any handful of Hill's pronunciamentos to his troops will convince the modern reader of the locution's validity (*Webster's:* "one who. . . murmurs, or grumbles; one who complains unreasonably").

Harvey Hill's great opportunity came on September 13–14 at the gaps in the South Mountain. Hill fought like a cornered tiger on the fourteenth, both personally and through his leadership, but he prepared slothfully and then reported on his performance immodestly and not entirely honestly. The North Carolinian's other pivotal involvement came through the loss of Lee's explicit blueprint for his army's far-flung maneuvers in Special Orders No. 191. The three members of the 27th Indiana who found the lost orders, inside what must be the three most famous cigars ever wrapped, turned the campaign around. The paper that they found was addressed to D. H. Hill and was a duplicate resulting from the nebulous affiliation of his division to each half of Lee's army. The emerging "corps" arrangement touted above as a significant adjustment seems even more important in light of the fact that the campaign's greatest disaster slipped through a poorly caulked seam between the de facto corps.

Hill probably was not directly culpable for the notorious "Lost Order," but he felt uneasy enough about his association with the matter to wedge his foot into his mouth about it. In the February 1868 issue of the magazine he published, *Land We Love* (an excellent and underutilized Confederate resource), Hill ostentatiously explained his innocence. Unwilling to let well enough alone, he then suggested that the Lost Order really worked altogether for the good because one of its subparagraphs contained outdated information. Longstreet no longer stood at Boonsboro, but instead had moved well to the northwest around Hagerstown. Harvey Hill postulated from this that McClellan's presumption that Longstreet lurked nearby caused him to be cautious—as though Little Mac ever needed encouragement in that line. When Hill's foolish theory caught R. E. Lee's eye on February 15, 1868, he commented on it about as harshly as Lee ever commented on anything. The quotes above about "queer temperament" and "he croaked" come from Lee's remarks at that time.

Lafayette McLaws had been a general officer for a year by September 1862, and a major general since spring, but he had been singularly uninvolved in any of the army's crucial moments during that time. In Maryland he found himself at the vortex in several instances and met the challenge in each case. His advance south down Maryland Heights overcame serious impediments and resulted in a major Confederate advantage. Subsequent difficulties in Pleasant Valley sometimes attributed to McLaws are more aptly charged elsewhere. Finally, on the field at Sharpsburg, McLaws's division achieved the most notable Confederate tactical triumph of the day.

Many of the important but lower ranking men who stood at the head of Southern brigades and regiments in September 1862 were nearing moments of high distinction; others had run out of steam or had reached levels of demonstrable incompetence. Robert E. Rodes of Virginia had attracted favorable attention at Seven Pines with his Alabama troops and would shine anew north of Turner's Gap. There on September 14 he took advantage of a network of abrupt lateral ridge fingers that compartmentalized Northern advances, giving him a chance to hold off what seemed like the entire Union army. A modern guide published for visitors in automobiles goes so far as to explain: "The terrain is very hilly and the roads prohibitive. It is not recommended that you try to explore the area." On that imposing ground Rodes proved himself again and gave promise of what he would do over the next two years.

Alfred H. Colquitt of Georgia became a brigadier general on September 1 and led his brigade two weeks later at Turner's Gap in South Mountain. Colquitt's name is familiar to modern students primarily because of his embarrassing failure at Chancellorsville, but in front of Turner's Gap the new general and his Georgians comported themselves with real distinction.

A few miles south of Turner's Gap at Crampton's Gap the brigade of little William Mahone stood forlornly in the path of a Federal juggernaut. Billy Mahone himself was absent nursing a wound suffered at Second Manassas. (It was this wound, reported to Mrs. Mahone as a "flesh wound," that elicited her familiar retort that William must be seriously hurt as he was so slender that he had no unimportant flesh to wound.) Colonel William Allen Parham of the 41st Virginia, known for some reason as "Gus," commanded in Mahone's absence. One of his subordinates said admiringly of Gus Parham that he was "the best curser when he chose I ever heard." Given the traditional conversational habits of armies since time immemorial, that is quite a tribute indeed. Swearing Gus held his regiments to their task at Crampton's with much fortitude and contributed notably to saving the army. Colonel Thomas T. Munford's 2nd Virginia Cavalry also fought at the gap in what Munford reported as a veritable Armageddon. The colonel added that precisely one of his men was killed in the action, which should help to clarify the differing perceptions of Civil War combat among mounted as opposed to dismounted men.

Howell Cobb also fought at Crampton's Gap, bringing his brigade to the action right at the crisis but completely losing control of it and contributing nothing to the defense. Raphael Moses of Longstreet's staff described Cobb as a jolly fellow memorable for his obesity and his good humor. As a result, Moses recalled, "when [Cobb] laughed he laughed all over, every particle of his avoirdupois shook like a jelly bag." The Georgia politician never fought with the Army of Northern Virginia again after the Maryland campaign.

Still another politician, like Colquitt and Cobb a Georgian, also left the army after this campaign. Robert A. Toombs had done appreciably more harm than good during his sojourn away from the political stump. Joseph L. Brent, who later would win his own wreath and stars as a Confederate general, wrote of encountering Toombs during the Seven Days and coming away from the conversation worried—until he remembered the prevailing wisdom that Toombs was "always excitable, and even extravagant in his declarations." General Toombs in the event performed well above the lower bridge at Sharpsburg, if not quite so well as he believed and loudly announced. Using September 17 as the centerpiece of an elaborate autobiographical bouquet, Toombs bowed out of the army with a flourish. His intemperate demeanor did not make him a popular hero in the Richmond political arena, but the high command of the army he left behind him must have been ecstatic at the change.

The Maryland campaign marked the end of the army's association with still another bewildered politician, Virginian Roger A. Pryor. During the Second Battle of Manassas, Pryor had disappeared for an interval and returned to tell an incredible tale of hiding out in a haystack between bouts of hand-to-hand bayonet combat. Whatever his prowess with edged weapons, Pryor was, to quote a cavalry colonel who observed him, quite simply "out of his element" in military situations. During the crisis around the Sunken Road and the Piper House, Pryor found himself thrust by succession into command of one of the largest veteran divisions on the field. His grasp did not begin to suffice for the situation, and the division dissolved as a military entity, though its well-tempered components functioned bravely. Lee transferred all of Pryor's regiments away from him soon after the battle, leaving this original secessionist a brigadier general without a brigade.

In June 1862 a captain in the 44th Georgia of Roswell S. Ripley's brigade referred to that general without discernible affection as "a big fat whiskey drinking loving man.'' A few weeks later Ripley led his brigade, subsequently famous as George Doles's, to disaster at Beaver Dam Creek. Ripley also was notable for his attitude toward the army commander. Not everyone viewed R. E. Lee with adulation, but Roswell Ripley was the only officer of much rank who openly hated him. Accordingly it is not surprising to note that Sharpsburg, where he suffered a wound, ended Ripley's connection with the Army of Northern Virginia.

Nathan G. Evans, known as ''Shanks'' in honor of his spindly underpinnings, qualified as one of the signal characters in an army full of them. His Prussian orderly, whom Evans called fondly his ''Barrelita,'' constantly attended the general with a gallon of whiskey in a barrel strapped to his back. Shanks Evans fought splendidly at First Manassas against daunting odds and won a well-deserved name for bravery in the process. Subsequently, however, Shanks spent enough energy drawing on his Barrelita's burden to prompt Tom Goree of Longstreet's staff to declare that Evans was ''nearly always under the influence of liquor.'' During the Ball's Bluff operation in October 1861, Eppa Hunton wrote that Evans was even ''a little drunker than usual.'' In September 1862, Shanks Evans had John Bell Hood under arrest as the outgrowth of an obscure quibble, complicating matters when the stalwart Hood was in requisition to lead his shock troops. Lee added Evans to the sizable list of men to be exiled quietly after the campaign.

Winfield Scott Featherston had led a sturdy Mississippi brigade for half a year without any striking success. Mild-mannered Cadmus M. Wilcox, though not much given to criticism or controversy, described General Featherston (and Pryor in the same phrase) as ''rather wild & inaccurate.'' Lee evidently agreed, because he sent Featherston away within a few months. He did the same to Brigadier General Thomas F. Drayton even before he dealt with Featherston. Drayton was a South Carolinian of high personal standing and also a personal friend of Jefferson Davis. The president's inevitable personal loyalty (witness his blind devotion to the much-loathed Commissary Lucius Northrop), combined with a chronic compulsion for dabbling with organization, made Lee write gingerly to Davis about Drayton. In one of his typically adroit letters to the fussy chief executive, Lee stated that, ''[Drayton] is a gentleman, and in his person a soldier, but seems to lack the capacity to command.''

Brigadier General John R. Jones performed with so little personal poise at Sharpsburg that he came under formal charges. In what must have been a unique and startling proceeding, this general officer of the legendary Army of Northern Virginia actually stood court-martial early in 1863 for personal cowardly behavior at Sharpsburg and elsewhere. The charges against Jones were so ''minute and lengthy'' that the army's general orders did not enumerate them; perhaps their volume served as a convenient veil to drop over an acute embarrassment. Stonewall Jackson had made Jones, a Virginia Military Institute graduate, one of his special projects, in the process displaying anew his much-mooted bad judgment in such things. The general jumped Jones from rank as a fairly junior field-grade officer all the way to brigadier general. Later Mighty Stonewall grumbled to one of his staff that putting one's trust in men was risky business. The verdict of Jones's court-martial finally appeared on April 18, 1863, acquitting him on each of several charges and specifications. Two weeks later, John R. Jones hurriedly left the battlefield of Chancellorsville and took himself out of the army without any further prompting. Jones added to his unusual record and reputation after the war by engaging, according to some accounts, in social arrangements unlike those normally expected from Confederate generals.

Two others of the army's leaders left service soon after Sharpsburg to the considerable detriment of the talent pool. Andrew Jackson Grigsby, colonel of the 27th Virginia and commander by seniority of the Stonewall Brigade, had served steadily and well. During the lull after Sharpsburg he resigned when Jackson promoted another of his projects—E. F. Paxton—from far down in the ranks over Grigsby's head. The disgusted word in the army was that Jackson disliked Grigsby's impious tendency to use vigorous language. Major General David Rumph Jones, known piquantly as Neighbor Jones, also fought his last for Lee near Antietam Creek. This Jones carried a solid reputation to the grave a few months later when heart trouble killed him.

Four other general officers died during the Maryland operations. Able, solid Samuel Garland was one of those young men too soon dead around whom conjecture still swirls about an ultimate level of competence. L. O'B. Branch survives through his own written words as a somewhat querulous fellow, but the brigade he had led for months was of fine quality that reflected favorably on its commander. George B. Anderson's mortal wound struck him at the high point of a young career, as he and his North Carolinians stood strong in the Sunken Road. William E. Starke had been a brigadier general for only one month when he died in the West Woods, without much chance to display his worth. The replacements for three of the four dead men—Alfred Iverson, James H. Lane, S. Dodson Ramseur, and Francis R. T. Nicholls, respectively—proved to be competent or better than competent. Even so, the army could ill afford the leadership drain.

The dead generals will not serve for comparison, but excluding them, no fewer than thirteen men who were leaders of brigades or divisions going into Maryland were washed out of the Army of Northern Virginia either at once or soon thereafter. None of the army's other campaigns equaled that purgative record, including even the shakedown cruise through the Seven Days.

Against the demonstrable failures exposed by the demands of battle must be reckoned such performances as those of Rodes, Colquitt, and Parham at South Mountain (enumerated above), and of such men as John Rogers Cooke, Richard B. Garnett, Jubal A. Early, William Barksdale, and Evander M. Law. Cooke marked himself as a man to watch when he led two small regiments in a surge that penetrated astoundingly deep into the Federal rear during the fight around the Sunken Road. Garnett enjoyed no opportunity for special distinction in Maryland but his mere presence in brigade command gave cause for optimism. Stonewall Jackson's rigid approach to Garnett's court-martial over events at Kernstown had left the senior officer at least as embarrassed as the junior, and now Garnett was back in the field, separated from Jackson and beginning an association with five Virginia regiments at the head of which he would die a famous death. Acerbic Jubal Early remained a brigadier general, but the notice he attracted at Cedar Mountain in August found further reason at Sharpsburg to count him as developing and dependable. William Barksdale had been a brigadier for only twenty-four days when he entered Maryland, but he steadily demonstrated that he would join Maxcy Gregg as that surprisingly rare creature, a fire-eating politician both willing and able to serve with distinction in the field. Brilliant young Evander M. Law led the deepest Confederate penetration into Miller's Cornfield with an élan that matched that of his famous chief, John B. Hood.

Personal performances aside, the Army of Northern Virginia fought about as well as it could possibly have done in the fields and woodlots above Antietam Creek, and better than anyone had any right to expect. In a perverse way, the splendid performance of his army highlights the degree to which Lee's determination to fight the battle must be adjudged one of his worst decisions of the war.

Federal cooperation contributed notably to Lee's escape from disaster at Sharpsburg. McClellan's indolence combined with Lee's interior lines to make possible Confederate juggling up and down the front to one point of crisis after another. No one who has written about the battle has failed to highlight the gradual and cautious Federal onset—on the right then the center then the left—in which each element waited almost courteously for its comrades to exit the stage. In fact, Northern tactics replicated that inept trait to a considerable degree all the way down the organizational chart. Not only did the sector attacks unfold seriatim rather than en masse, but so in many cases did corps attacks within sectors, division attacks within corps, and even brigade attacks within divisions.

In the early morning advance of the Federal First Corps, for instance, James B. Ricketts's division received orders to advance into Miller's Cornfield with all three brigades. Abram Duryea's brigade moved promptly and with at least temporary good effect. George L. Hartsuff went down, hard hit by a shell fragment, and it understandably took some time for the senior colonel, Richard Coulter, who assumed command, to bring Hartsuff's brigade back under control and lead it forward. Colonel William A. Christian, commanding the third brigade of Ricketts's division, began to advance in good time, but the colonel found the fire coming against the brigade more than he could stand and he scampered to the rear. Colonel Peter Lyle ably undertook to straighten out the mess, but by the time he succeeded the brigade moved into a cauldron in which

Duryea and Coulter had already peaked and ebbed. Ricketts's sizable force could hardly be counted a functioning division under the circumstances, and the three brigades constituted something less than the sum of their parts.

In addition to interior lines and Union cooperation, the Army of Northern Virginia benefited from good ground. Military forces that choose their own ground (in most cases the defensive army) gain the advantage of picking the best available terrain. Some of the heaviest fighting at Sharpsburg developed at short range and on level fields offering little advantage to either side. Several key locations, however, benefited Lee's defense. Nicodemus Heights and its southerly extension into Hauser's Ridge offered admirable artillery anchors. Federal toleration of Confederate control of Nicodemus Heights remains one of the mysteries of the battle. S. D. Lee's ridge opposite the Dunker Church provided another critical artillery aerie. The Sunken Road that turned into the Bloody Lane made possible long and crucial defense of the center. Commanding ground, including some ready-made bunkers in the form of a rock quarry, combined with another generous dose of Northern ennui to make Rohrbach Bridge impregnable for vital hours.

To good ground the Confederates occasionally added some monumental good luck. The thunderous disaster into which Edwin V. Sumner and John Sedgwick stumbled in the West Woods, which must be adjudged the Southerners' brightest moment on the day, can be explained in part in terms of Federal tactical mistakes. The apparently beautifully orchestrated Confederate execution that plucked that golden opportunity, however, included more of good fortune than of deft forethought. The gods of war who frowned on Lee in vectoring Special Orders No. 191 to its final unfriendly destination smiled on him then as fragments of four Southern divisions popped up in the right place around the West Woods at the right time.

On more than one occasion during September 17, 1862, Lee's fate lay in the hands of a few good men who hung on to precarious positions with grit difficult to imagine but easy to admire. The Alabama and North Carolina troops under Robert E. Rodes and George B. Anderson who christened Bloody Lane with their lifeblood probably saved the army. When Rodes and Anderson could do no more, Longstreet's staff personally served guns a few hundred yards behind the lane. Those half dozen young officers constituted the final paper-thin defense in that sector until Harvey Hill rounded up a few score stragglers as an emergency fire brigade. As the battle rolled on into the outskirts of Sharpsburg, shattered batteries put together little one-gun detachments to send back into the breach, and brigades the size of companies stumbled into gaps that warranted defense by twenty times their numbers.

Some of the most desperate Confederate fighting at Sharpsburg focused on a modestly dimensioned pasture that abutted the south edge of Miller's Cornfield. The carnage in the Cornfield promptly, by a sort of secular transubstantiation, turned that theretofore ordinary farm lot into one of the awesome and sacred names in the nation's military lexicon. By far the largest portion of the Southerners engaged on that end of the field, however, fought from positions in the adjacent pasture, not in the corn. The Pasture never attained the status of a separate geographical feature for one reason or another, but recognition of its role will aid careful students in understanding the battle.

The forty-acre pie-shaped wedge of the Pasture ran more than six hundred yards north and south along the east edge of the Hagerstown Pike. Across its northern extent the Pasture stretched about five hundred yards along the Cornfield and reached to the East Woods. The apex of the pie-shaped wedge, at its southern extremity, was formed by the junction of the Hagerstown Pike and the Smoketown Road directly opposite the Dunker Church. The Pasture served as the combat front line during the early morning fight for Confederate brigades commanded by Marcellus Douglass, J. A. Walker, Harry T. Hays, Ripley, Colquitt, and D. K. McRae. Hood's two brigades under William T. Wofford and Law also swept through the Pasture en route to the Cornfield, into which they made the only really substantial Confederate penetration. Later, troops under Joseph B. Kershaw and Manning and others fought through the Pasture's southern apex.

The unflinching determination of his troops in the Pasture and in Bloody Lane and all across the famous landscape surrounding Sharpsburg served Lee well. So did good ground, Union listlessness, interior lines, and one important injection of random good luck. The combination left R. E. Lee intact at sunset on September 17, defiantly facing McClellan's host with a handful of exhausted men, the mighty Potomac River at his back. Lee has been criticized for standing firm through September 18 with a shrunken and battered army that stood in real danger of destruction. He is even more vulnerable to criticism for choosing to stand at Sharpsburg on September 16 and 17.

That Lee needed to raid north of the Potomac can hardly be doubted. He was obliged to seek a situation in which the exigencies of war favored his army, and then strike in a setting that offered not only immediate rewards but the chance to reap major fruits of a victory. Once into Maryland, however, when the unmistakable impact of acute straggling became apparent in his army, Lee faced a new combination of factors. When Special Orders No. 191 dropped into McClellan's lap and Lee learned of that unhappy event almost immediately—the odds mounted even more steeply against the Southern army. The valor and skill displayed by Confederate officers and men around Sharpsburg saved their army from disaster, but no remotely reasonable scenario can now be offered nor could then have been constructed that afforded Lee the chance to do what he had crossed the river to accomplish.

Employing hindsight, that luxurious but largely illegitimate historical tool, we can say unequivocally that Lee should not have attacked on the third day at Gettysburg; that he should not have let the army get out of hand at Malvern Hill; that the tete-de-pont at Rappahannock Station was not such a good idea. None of those things, however, was an inevitable and patently apparent result. In each of those instances and most others during the war, Lee chose among a sometimes painfully slender group of alternatives, but alternatives that offered at least potential for success. Lee himself said in response to some after-the-fact criticism: "After it is all over, as stupid a fellow as I am can see the mistakes that were made. I notice, however, that my mistakes are never told me until it is too late. . . ."

The salient difference between Lee's decision to stand at Sharpsburg and most others that he made during the war is that at that time and place, and with the shrunken numbers available to him, Lee simply could not accomplish anything. Had McClellan literally—instead of only figuratively—abandoned the field to the Confederates, Lee could have done nothing more than follow his enemy back toward Frederick in meek impotence. For the only time during the war until its closing months, Lee did not have the resources to exploit any opening, no matter how appetizing. That the Army of Northern Virginia fought brilliantly to attain a precarious tactical draw is vivid evidence of the poverty of Lee's strategic decision.

As the battle developed, its primary result was to drain some of the best blood of Lee's army into the soil of Washington County, Maryland. Perhaps the Southern blood that drenched the fields around Gettysburg and Chancellorsville accomplished no more in the long run, but it was shed in operations that bore the hopeful seeds of victory and independence. To study Sharpsburg from a Confederate perspective, then, is to study a fascinating story of fighting prowess and of sturdy determination, but not of Southern nationhood trembling in the balance. Among the higher ranks, by contrast, Sharpsburg was a stern crucible in which the fire of battle separated gold from dross, completing a process begun a few weeks before in the Seven Days campaign.

On the afternoon of September 15, as weary Confederates climbed westward out of the Antietam Creek bottom, Lee met them and moved among them providing encouragement. When men of James L. Kemper's brigade approached the forming Southern line on what would become the battlefield, Lee pointed ahead of them and said, "We will make our stand on those hills." His decision to make that stand was a bad one, probably his worst of the war.

A. WILSON GREENE

"I Fought the Battle Splendidly"
George B. McClellan
and the Maryland Campaign

Generations of Civil War students have warmly debated the conduct and significance of the 1862 Maryland campaign. Among all the contested aspects of this pivotal military operation, the controversy swirls most tempestuously around the Federal commander, Major General George Brinton McClellan.

Some historians view the thirty-five-year-old Philadelphian's performance in a positive light. "Nowhere has [a] charge of slowness been less justly levelled," argues Joseph Harsh. "On September 2, 1862, McClellan assumed command of the disorganized, dispirited and chaotically intermingled fragments of five separate armies. Within one week, he marched into Maryland with a field army which was still sorting out its wagons and batteries and leavened by a high percentage of raw troops snatched directly from the mustering-in ceremonies. In another week he brought Lee to bay at Antietam Creek and inflicted upon him the severest casualty rate ever suffered by the Army of Northern Virginia in the bloodiest day's battle of the entire war."

Francis Palfrey, writing with shorter hindsight, evaluates Little Mac more critically: "Of McClellan's conduct of the battle there is little to be said in the way of praise beyond the fact that he did fight it voluntarily, without having it forced upon him." General Peter S. Michie is less charitable still. "It does not seem possible to find any other battle ever fought," insists Michie, "in the conduct of which more errors were committed than are clearly attributable to the commander of the Army of the Potomac."

How did McClellan rate his own performance amid the rolling hills of Frederick and Washington counties? "Those in whose judgment I rely," admitted the Young Napoleon, "tell me that I fought the battle splendidly and that it was a masterpiece of art."

Sitting at his breakfast table in the frenzied Federal capital on the first Tuesday of September, McClellan could hardly have predicted that within a fortnight he would preside over the most important engagement of the Civil War.

For at that moment, he presided over precious little, having been reduced in a matter of months from general-in-chief of all Union armies to the titular director of the Washington defense force. The disappointing results of his Peninsula campaign, which McClellan laid at the feet of the Republican administration, explained his rapid fall from grace. Now, two representatives of that faithless political cabal interrupted his morning meal. President Abraham Lincoln, accompanied by the current general-in-chief, Henry W. Halleck, asked McClellan, as a personal favor, to take control of the dejected army John Pope had left in the wake of Second Manassas. Lincoln did this not from any illusion that McClellan offered an expectation of battlefield genius. Rather, as he told his private secretary, "There is no man in the Army who can man these fortifications and lick these troops of ours into shape half as well as he. . . . If he can't fight himself, he excels in making others ready to fight."

Although the president thus cherished hope for only limited achievements from McClellan, the general confided to his wife that he had been called upon to accomplish nothing less than "the salvation of the nation." In either case, McClellan's appointment reinspired the Army of the Potomac, instantly vindicating Lincoln's decision. "From extreme sadness we passed in a twinkling to a delirium of delight," remembered one soldier; "a Deliverer had come." Not only did the morale of the army undergo an astonishing change, but Little Mac also remolded the disparate divisions of his own, Pope's, and Ambrose E. Burnside's commands into an integrated military machine. This transformation occurred almost literally overnight, but McClellan felt that the long refitting process had but barely begun. Then, suddenly, events beyond his control changed the rules of the game.

Robert E. Lee's movement across the Potomac signaled the continuation of a Confederate offensive that had commenced ten weeks earlier along the Chickahominy during the Seven Days. Clearly the situation now demanded a campaign in the field, and Lincoln, for a second time, turned to Ambrose Burnside. Burnside, for a second time, turned away. The loyal and appropriately self-effacing Hoosier-turned-Rhode Islander humbly recommended that the president stick with McClellan. Facing a military crisis and with no practical alternative, Lincoln visited McClellan's residence and assigned him responsibility for meeting Lee's threat. After the war, Little Mac claimed that he never received an official imprimature to leave the capital's fortifications. "I . . . fought the battles of South Mountain and Antietam with a halter around my neck," wrote the general. "If the Army of the Potomac had been defeated and I had survived I would, no doubt, have been tried for assuming authority without orders and . . . probably have been condemned to death." T. Harry Williams calls this assertion "pure romance. He either forgot the conference at his house with Lincoln, or he was lying. It is hard to see how he could have forgotten the meeting."

Major General Ambrose Everett Burnside

In any event, McClellan began to move on September 5, albeit with great reluctance. "Nothing but sheer necessity justified the advance of the Army of the Potomac," asserted the general, who decried the supposedly woeful material and emotional well-being of his men. Burnside marched on the right in charge of a wing that included Jesse Reno's Ninth and Joseph Hooker's First Corps. Edwin V. Sumner, the Old Bull of the Woods, took the center with his Second Corps and the Twelfth Corps, temporarily under Alpheus S. Williams.

William B. Franklin led the left wing consisting of his Sixth Corps and Darius N. Couch's division of the Fourth Corps. McClellan's entire army numbered eighty thousand troops with almost that many more left behind to protect Washington. Little Mac personally departed the capital on September 7 and established headquarters in Rockville, Maryland.

The army progressed at a glacial pace, covering an average of just six miles per day between Washington and Frederick. McClellan's desire to proceed with his reorganization partially explains his hesitancy to test the legs of his soldiers. Moreover, no one could be sure of Lee's intentions. The Federal cavalry proved unable to ascertain the enemy's whereabouts, and back in Washington, Halleck fretted overmuch for the safety of the capital. Old Brains, who at age forty-seven met neither of his moniker's criteria, sent numerous messages to McClellan expressing his conviction that the Confederate occupation of Maryland was merely a ruse. Lee's actual objective, warned Halleck, remained the capture of Washington from south of the Potomac. "I was more than once cautioned that I was moving too rashly and exposing the capital to an attack from the Virginia side," recalled Little Mac.

Had McClellan's track record been one of lightning marches, it would be easy to ascribe the army's snaillike advance solely to Halleck's hand-wringing. In truth, the general-in-chief's insistence upon maintaining McClellan's left firmly on the Potomac and his continual whining about exposing Washington dovetailed snugly with McClellan's natural inclinations.

Halleck's enfeebled military judgment affected the Maryland campaign in a more important regard—in fact, it helped create the large stage on which the drama would be played. McClellan, no slouch at whining in his own right, solicited reinforcements from Halleck within days after leaving Washington. One obvious source of additional manpower would be the Federal garrison at Harpers Ferry, whose position at the confluence of the Shenandoah and Potomac rivers was compromised while Lee roamed about western Maryland. But Halleck refused to withdraw the twelve thousand men stationed at the Ferry and nearby Martinsburg. Instead, he instructed McClellan to go to the relief of Colonel Dixon S. Miles's force, ignoring Little Mac's well-founded objections.

Ironically, Lee viewed the Yankees at Harpers Ferry as an unacceptable threat to his supply line. On September 9, he ordered the division of his army to reduce Miles's command. The Confederate chieftain willingly assumed this risk, based in part on his knowledge of McClellan. "He is an able general but a very cautious one," Lee told John G. Walker. "His army. . .will not be prepared for offensive operations—or he will not think it so—for three or four weeks. Before that time I hope to be on the Susquehanna."

While the Army of Northern Virginia subdivided amoebalike, Miles sat tight at Harpers Ferry, and McClellan crawled toward the crossroads at Frederick. The townsfolk of that loyal city greeted the Union army with a tumultuous welcome as the blue vanguard arrived on September 12. "I can't describe to you for want of time the enthusiastic reception we met with . . . at Frederick," McClellan wrote his wife.

As joyful as the Young Napoleon's appearance made the good citizens of Frederick, the Federal commander still operated under two crippling handicaps, one external and one self-imposed. First, Halleck persisted in his unreasonable fear for Washington's security. Referring not to Stonewall Jackson's developing encirclement of Harpers Ferry, but to the phantom gray legions lurking about the Virginia forts, Old Brains wired McClellan on September 13, "Until you know more certainly the enemy's forces south of the Potomac, you are wrong in thus uncovering the capital." This was nonsense and McClellan knew it. Lee's whole army, not a diversionary detachment, had entered the Free State. Determining the accurate size of that army, however, posed more serious problems for Little Mac.

McClellan's trusted but untrustworthy spy master, Allan Pinkerton, had no network in Maryland, so the Union commander relied upon General Alfred Pleasonton and the Federal cavalry to specify Lee's strength. Pinkerton had reported on August 10 that two hundred thousand Rebels were under arms in northern Virginia. A month later, Pleasonton adjusted that outrageous estimate downward some 40 percent, still a ludicrous exaggeration of Confederate manpower. McClellan informed Halleck on September 11 that all the "evidence that has been accumulated from various sources since we left Washington goes to prove most conclusively that the entire rebel army in Virginia, amounting to not less than 120,000 men, is in the vicinity of Frederick. . . . If we should be defeated the consequences to the country would be disastrous in the extreme." This was vintage McClellan, as was his renewed request for additional troops from Washington. Halleck released Fitz John Porter's Fifth Corps on September 12, but unnecessarily retained both the Third and Eleventh corps around the capital. Nevertheless, Porter's presence would raise the actual numerical odds against Lee to more than two-to-one.

McClellan's willingness to accept Pleasonton's information, gleaned from naive villagers and boastful prisoners, is only marginally less unpardonable than his facile confidence that the Richmond government could arm and equip greater forces than those of the United States. One writer, in fact, suggests that McClellan could not have honestly endorsed what he reported to Halleck: "It is impossible . . . that McClellan believed that . . . in Maryland the Confederates had the forces he attributed to them," says Palfrey. "If he did believe it, he ought, with his knowledge of their fighting qualities, to have abandoned offensive operations and thrown his army behind fortifications constructed to protect Washington, Baltimore, and Philadelphia, and waited for more troops." The sad truth appears to be, however, that Little Mac did assume Lee outnumbered him in Maryland, an opinion predicated, as Michie says, on "an unaccountable weakness in McClellan's mental equipment. . . . '' Under these circumstances, Little Mac might indeed have drawn a defensive cordon east of the mountains had not he stumbled across one of the most extraordinary strokes of fortune in American military history.

Special Orders No. 191, outlining Lee's entire plan and revealing the vulnerable dispositions of the scattered Confederate divisions, handed McClellan the strategic initiative on a silver platter. "Here is a paper with which if I cannot whip Bobbie Lee, I will be willing to go home," the general beamed, unconscious of the ironic prophecy of his words. "I think Lee has made a gross mistake, and that he will be severely punished for it," he wired the president. "I have all the plans of the rebels, and will catch them in their own trap if my men are equal to the emergency." Any military context that required McClellan to move with celerity certainly qualified as an emergency, but asking the rank and file of the Union army to meet it would not be the rub—it never was. Eighteen hours elapsed before the first Northern soldier marched in response to the intelligence bonanza contained in Special Orders No. 191. The Federal commander spent the interim studying his maps, contemplating Lee's vast legions, and slowly adjusting to the new situation.

A curious dichotomy exists in this campaign between McClellan's bold rhetoric, which seemingly displayed a firm understanding of strategic objectives, and his actual performance on the field. Was McClellan's promise to send trophies of triumph to Lincoln a patronizing gesture designed to tell the administration what it wanted to hear, or a metaphor for action that when executed would result in Lee's annihilation? Was McClellan sincere when he characterized his advance toward South Mountain as "rapid and vigorous," or was this merely transparent apologia?

Every writer agrees that Little Mac erred egregiously when he failed to order an immediate march toward the west on the afternoon of September 13. Two important possibilities beckoned seductively to an energized Federal army. By breaking through Crampton's Gap on his left, McClellan might have overwhelmed Lafayette McLaws's force in Pleasant Valley and seized Maryland Heights, thus relieving Harpers Ferry. An offensive thrust through Turner's Gap and Boonsboro on the Union right would have isolated D. H. Hill and James Longstreet from Jackson's forces south of the Potomac, creating the opportunity to crush a wing of Lee's army.

Instead, McClellan squandered the afternoon and evening of the thirteenth, sending orders after dark for a two-pronged advance the next morning. He told Franklin that he intended "to cut the enemy in two and beat him in detail," and called on his lieutenant to employ all his "intellect and the utmost activity," but Little Mac declined to unleash his army for nearly a day.

Warren W. Hassler and other sympathetic biographers suggest that McClellan's caution on September 13 emerged from his belief that both D. H. Hill and

Longstreet occupied Boonsboro, as indicated in Special Orders No. 191. Crediting this portion of the Confederate army with thirty thousand men, Little Mac wished to avoid a precipitant march against such a formidable foe. This reasoning, however, discounted a substantial body of intelligence that accurately placed Longstreet's two divisions at Hagerstown. In reality, only D. H. Hill lay in a position to contest the nothernmost gaps. The Confederates held Crampton's Gap even more tenuously, and Franklin could have easily captured it by nightfall. Any thoughtful analysis of Special Orders No. 191, which provided the organization and distribution of the Confederate army, should have revealed Southern vulnerability, but no such evaluation occurred. Instead, McClellan arbitrarily inflated the size of Lee's divisions by a factor of three. His only positive act on the thirteenth resulted in the occupation of the Middletown Valley by portions of the Ninth Corps, who built fires in the evening that disclosed their presence and sacrificed the element of surprise.

McClellan tossed aside a great opportunity on September 13, before a trigger had been pulled in the campaign. This would not be the last time a Union commander gained the early advantage over Lee only to lose it—Burnside at Fredericksburg and Hooker at Chancellorsville would do so as well—but at no time would the stakes be so high. The Army of the Potomac confronted a rare chance to win a cheap and decisive victory, but as Stephen Sears says, their leader was ''the captain who would not dare.''

McClellan remained at Frederick on the morning of September 14, cantering forward along the National Road later in the day to watch the fighting at Fox's and Turner's gaps from the foot of the mountain. The general acted with regal detachment, occasionally pointing theatrically toward the smoky aeries where Reno and Hooker struggled against determined Confederates and rugged terrain. His men indulged in extravagant demonstrations of affection for their commander, despite the fact that his previous day's hesitation allowed Longstreet to reinforce the beleaguered D. H. Hill. The Federal attacks at the northern gaps suffered from a lack of tactical coordination. By nightfall, however, the Southerners occupied an untenable position and withdrew through the darkness. Franklin conducted his dilatory approach to Crampton's Gap according to the McClellan manual. He appeared to be satisfied with merely seizing the village at the base of South Mountain until division commander Henry W. Slocum brushed aside the token Confederate line on the eastern slope and wrested the crest from a single Rebel brigade.

The victories at South Mountain evinced no battlefield brilliance and arrived half a day too late to produce dramatic results. Nevertheless, the Yankees displayed uncharacteristic swiftness. ''I thought I knew McClellan,'' confessed T. J. Jackson, ''but this movement of his puzzles me.'' With Lee's mountain barrier in Federal hands, McClellan might still rescue Miles at Harpers Ferry, catch Lee north of the Potomac with a divided army, or both. Speed and determination now counted more than ever.

McClellan's correspondence on September 15 again reveals that strange contradiction between his words and his deeds. At 8:00 A.M. he wired Halleck that the army was in hot pursuit of the invaders and would hurry everything forward "to press their retreat to the utmost." Ninety minutes later he wrote to his wife in the same vein: "I am pushing everything after them with the greatest rapidity and expect to gain great results. . . . "

The army did snake down the west slope at early dawn, although its commander stayed in the Middletown Valley directing events from the rear. Franklin's mission to relieve Harpers Ferry by dislodging McLaws from Maryland Heights failed miserably. The left-wing commander encountered a thin line of Confederates drawn across Pleasant Valley between South Mountain and Elk Ridge. Franklin now echoed McClellan's improbable concern for the safety of his own rear, threatened, supposedly, by the flying remnants of the Turner's Gap defenders. He also shared Little Mac's assessment of Rebel firepower, reporting that he opposed twice his number. McClellan acquiesced in these fictions and permitted Franklin's three divisions to idle away the day while McLaws played an unimpeded role in Harpers Ferry's capitulation.

Meanwhile, the Union right and center wings, comprising thirty-five brigades of infantry and Pleasonton's cavalry, rolled down the National and Old Sharpsburg roads. The Ninth Corps departed Fox's Gap at noon, after an unnecessary delay that would provide McClellan the grist for blaming Burnside for the day's empty results. In truth, the bulk of the Federal army poured directly into Boonsboro from Turner's Gap, but progressed only to Keedysville by midafternoon. Sumner assumed control of the advanced elements of the army until McClellan reined up about 3:00 P.M. The wild cheering that greeted the commander on his ride to the front may explain his languid pace, but not that of the army itself. The roads between Turner's Gap, Boonsboro, and Sharpsburg were good, and the ground on both sides favorable for parallel columns. But no one pressed the blue brigades beyond the leisurely gait that had characterized their march from Washington.

Edwin V. Sumner eagerly indicated the Rebel lines across Antietam Creek where Lee had taken refuge with some fifteen thousand troops. After a "rapid examination," McClellan reacted like an artillery subaltern, personally directing the placement of his batteries. He then massed his arriving infantry along the Boonsboro Pike, thus delaying any deployment into line of battle. There would be no need for a battle line, however, because on September 15 there would be no battle. Deciding that the hour had grown too late to launch an attack, McClellan told his subordinates that he would defer any action until the morrow.

The Union commander knew that he confronted a mere fraction of the Army of Northern Virginia on September 15. None of the units associated with the Harpers Ferry operation could possibly have been at Sharpsburg. Even Little Mac's creative arithmetic should have disclosed that he had trapped Lee in inferior strength with his back against the Potomac. Yet McClellan disdained the offensive. Why? The answer may be found by considering McClellan's curious view of the campaign. As we have seen, the Union commander gave evidence in his correspondence that he hoped to "gain great results" as a consequence of the action on South Mountain. On the other hand, in McClellan's mind, the Federal army had already accomplished much, perhaps all, that he intended to ask of it. From his headquarters west of Middletown, the general informed Halleck that the Rebel army had been "shockingly whipped" and had suffered fifteen thousand casualties at the gaps. McClellan wrote even more explicitly to his wife, telling Ellen he had "just learned that the enemy are retreating in a panic and that our victory is complete. How glad I am for my country that it is delivered from immediate peril. . . . "

President Lincoln, pacing nervously at the War Department, rejoiced at the news of the fighting at South Mountain. "God bless you, and all with you," enthused Lincoln, "destroy the rebel army, if possible." McClellan accepted the praise willingly enough, but deferred the destruction.

Jacob Cox, heir to the command of the Ninth Corps following Reno's mortal wounding at Fox's Gap, "confidently expected a battle" on September 16. Instead, the Union army passed the day in tedious inaction. Promising Halleck that he would "attack as soon as the situation of the enemy is developed," Little Mac bustled about in the morning haze reconnoitering the ground and evaluating the enemy's dispositions, but he took no steps to prepare an assault.

Shortly after noon, McClellan circulated orders scheduling the offensive for the seventeenth. He consumed the remainder of the day "finding fords, clearing the approaches, and hurrying up the ammunition and supply trains" which, McClellan dubiously asserted, "had been delayed by the rapid march of the troops. . . . " Thus, the Army of the Potomac wasted yet another turn of the earth while the Army of Northern Virginia gradually reunited on the right bank of Antietam Creek.

Little Mac's refusal to move on September 16 sprang from a familiar trio of factors. He told Ellen this day that he had "no doubt delivered Penna. and Maryland," implying that barring the gray hordes from Harrisburg and Baltimore represented triumph enough, the president's wishes notwithstanding. Moreover, if the Peninsula campaign and its antecedents revealed anything about McClellan, it was that he would not budge until he deemed his army fully prepared. He renounced the possibility that Lee might use the period of grace to improve his defensive arrangements, on either side of the Potomac. Finally, McClellan reckoned he faced three or four times the 26,500 Confederates in line on September 16, an exaggeration shared by his confidants at headquarters. Under these circumstances, therefore, would it not be best to gather all the Union divisions east of the Antietam, carefully distribute artillery to repulse an attack, and permit Lee the time to skulk back to Virginia burdened by the stigma of a failed invasion?

A bloodless victory of manuever, the quintessence of military accomplishment for McClellan, was not destined at Sharpsburg. The Young Napoleon afforded Lee every chance to admit defeat, but the Confederate commander would not cooperate. Rebel cannon roared defiantly from across Antietam Creek on September 16, and McClellan prepared at last to offer battle. He issued no written orders for his assaults and held no council of war to articulate his plan. Such a lack of orchestration suggests a certain irresolution in McClellan, born of his obvious reluctance to fight Lee and his general incapacity to craft a tactical offensive under any but the most favorable circumstances.

McClellan provides conflicting expositions of his arrangements in two official reports and his postwar memoirs. Writing four weeks after the battle he relates that the ''design was to make the main attack upon the enemy's left—at least to create a diversion in favor of the main attack, with the hope of something more by assailing the enemy's right—and, as soon as one or both of the flank movements were fully successful, to attack their center with any reserve I might then have on hand.'' His final report, written almost a year later and published in 1864, modified his earlier explanation, particularly in regard to the movement against Lee's right. ''My plan for the impending general engagement was to attack the enemy's left with the corps of Hooker and Mansfield, supported by Sumner's, and if necessary by Franklin's, and as soon as matters looked favorably there to move the corps of Burnside against the enemy's extreme right upon the ridge running to the south and the rear of Sharpsburg, and having carried their position, to pass along the crest toward our right, and whenever either of these flank movements should be successful, to advance our center with all the forces then disposable.''

Reconciling these two specimens of labyrinthian prose leaves just one matter clear: McClellan intended to hit Lee with a right hook. Burnside's role is less certain. Was his mission a diversion or a full-scale attack? Would it come simultaneously with Hooker's assault or subsequent to it? Jacob Cox testifies that his assignment closely reflected a conservative interpretation of what McClellan wrote in his preliminary report. ''Certainly the assumption that the Ninth Corps could cross the Antietam alone at the only place on the field where the Confederates had their line immediately upon the stream,'' wrote Cox, ''which must be crossed under fire by two narrow heads of column, and could then turn to the right along the high ground occupied by the hostile army before that army had been broken or seriously shaken elsewhere, is one which would hardly be made till time had dimmed the remembrance of the actual positions of Lee's divisions upon the field.''

When his flanking efforts had achieved an unspecified degree of success,

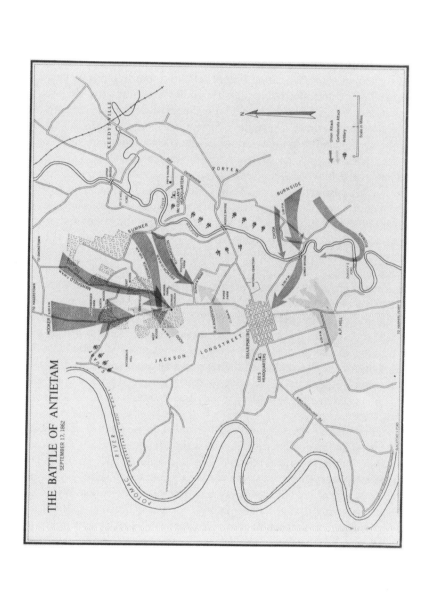

THE BATTLE OF ANTIETAM
SEPTEMBER 17, 1862

Little Mac would then unfetter his reserves in the center. The question here would be the general's conception of success and his ability to assess the enemy's condition. Would nothing less than the complete rout of Lee's army be the prerequisite for action, or would an orderly retirement or signs of exhaustion and imminent collapse qualify? Did McClellan possess the reservoir of moral courage necessary to commit "all the forces then disposable"?

Despite the nebulous character of McClellan's plan—one that had not fully crystallized even in retrospect—it might have pulverized the Army of Northern Virginia. In fact, virtually any plausible scheme could have created such an outcome. Lee's flanks were vulnerable, his center weak, and he husbanded few reserves. The Potomac flowed in his rear, and his line of retreat depended on Boteler's (also known as Blackford's) Ford. A breakthrough on any portion of Lee's perimeter, if vigorously exploited, could spell disaster for the Confederates. An adequate battle plan, however, must be adequately executed. McClellan's decision to suspend his offensive on September 15–16 shortened the odds against Lee. Moreover, organizational matters within the Army of the Potomac boded ill.

McClellan abruptly and without explanation abandoned his wing system on the eve of battle. Because of Hooker's success at Turner's Gap, the Federal leader selected the First Corps to spearhead the main attack, supported by the Twelfth Corps. Curiously, McClellan thus designated Irvin McDowell's and Nathaniel P. Banks's old units from Pope's army, troops supposedly suffering physical and spiritual trauma, to land the primary blow. This removed Hooker from Burnside's command and the Twelfth Corps, now under newly arrived J. K. F. Mansfield, from Sumner's control. McClellan's tampering left Sumner frustrated, but cut Old Burn to the quick. Little Mac offered no rationale for his reshuffling and took no steps to soothe the bruised egos of his deposed wing commanders. It is hard to imagine Robert E. Lee neglecting to consider the human element if military necessity dictated an eleventh-hour demotion of his lieutenants. McClellan's refusal to do this left the disgruntled Burnside thinking like a wing commander with no wing, and would contribute to the next day's problems on the left.

Worst of all, McClellan tipped his hand on the afternoon and evening of September 16 when he sent Hooker across the Upper Bridge. "It was now evident," wrote a brigade commander in John Bell Hood's division, "that the enemy had effected a crossing entirely to our left, and that he would make the attack on that wing early in the morning. . . . " Lee adjusted his lines and actually engaged Hooker's lead units in an indecisive firefight at dusk. The flank attack Little Mac envisioned would degenerate into a frontal charge the next morning.

Once in position on the right bank of the Antietam, Hooker urged McClellan to send him immediate reinforcements. McClellan, however, waited until after sunset to dispatch Mansfield, whose Twelfth Corps stumbled across the creek near midnight to settle into a dripping bivouac a mile in Hooker's rear. Sumner received instructions only to prepare his Second Corps for a crossing the following morning. McClellan's lack of coordination and piecemeal commitment set the tone for the war's bloodiest day.

The Union assaults on the morning of September 17, 1862, provide Americans with some of their most chilling geographic images—the West Woods, Miller's

Major General Joseph Hooker

Cornfield, the Sunken Road. The unspeakable chaos that raged across those pastoral places has grown synonymous with the sanguinary futility of the Civil War, for when the smoke cleared and the guns fell silent, neither side had gained an advantage. Victory on the right, however, dangled within reach of the Federals all day. They enjoyed greater numbers, more powerful artillery, and the tactical initiative. What went wrong?

When evaluating the conduct of a battle, it is important to remember the unique function of each level of command. In simplest terms, the ranking officer bears responsibility for bringing his units to the battlefield at the right times and in the right places. He must communicate his objectives to his subordinates and be prepared to provide personal inspiration at crucial moments. The actual combat is directed by subordinates, who, consistent with their overall mission, must react to changing battlefield conditions. The best chieftains create a climate in which boldness and innovation are valued commodities; the best executive officers exercise those qualities.

The battle of Antietam exemplifies the costly results that accrue to generals who fail at both levels. While George B. McClellan is answerable for lost opportunities between September 13 and 16, he shares with his corps commanders the onus for lost opportunities on the day of battle. Little Mac set the stage for disappointment on the Federal right by neglecting to articulate his vision of events and by failing to designate a clear chain of command in this sector. Consequently, when wounds removed Hooker and Mansfield from the scene, their successors possessed no firm conception of the situation and no single source to guide them. The First, Twelfth, and Second corps acted without concert, McClellan staggering their movement across the Antietam. Warren W. Hassler suggests that the general did so better to facilitate an all-out attack at dawn. But Little Mac never ordered such an assault. In fact, he deliberately prevented an impatient Sumner from crossing the creek with his lead division until hours after Hooker pitched into Jackson.

''Could Hooker and Mansfield have acted together,'' writes Cox, ''or, still better, could Sumner's Second Corps have marched before day and united with the first onset,—Lee's left must inevitably have been crushed long before the Confederate divisions of McLaws, Walker, and A. P. Hill could have reached the field. It is this failure to carry out any intelligible plan which the historian must regard as the unpardonable military fault on the National side.'' ''To account for the hours between 4 and 8 that morning,'' concludes Cox, ''is the most serious responsibility of the National commander.''

To be sure, Hooker and Mansfield should have attacked in concert and could have done so without McClellan's specific approval. Moreover, Fighting Joe disregarded the key terrain on Nicodemus Heights, the capture of which would have compromised Lee's defense. But it is puzzling to ponder how McClellan, calmly observing the morning fight through a telescope and rings of cigar smoke at his rear-area headquarters, could reject the principle of mass in his attacks. Had Lee actually commanded the number of men his opponent credited to him, Little Mac's piecemeal commitment would have done to the entire Army of the Potomac what Edwin Sumner did to John Sedgwick's division.

The Old Bull of the Woods craved action on September 17. He had stomped around the Pry House since early dawn waiting for the green light from his superior. After the battle, Sumner told a congressional committee, "I have always believed that, instead of sending these troops into action in driblets, had General McClellan authorized me to march these forty thousand on the left flank of the enemy, we could not have failed to throw them right back in front of the divisions of our army on the left." Sumner's judgment is correct. McClellan's partisans argue that three corps committed simultaneously would have bumbled into one another to no advantage, but adequate room existed for deploying such a force between the Joseph Poffenberger farm and the southern end of the East Woods. The Union army consisted of the right stuff for such a coordinated thrust.

Unfortunately, a combination of Sumner's impetuosity and McClellan's timidity conspired against the Second Corps. Hood's 7:00 a.m. appearance at the Cornfield prompted Little Mac to order Sumner forward within thirty minutes. However, he retained a third of Sumner's firepower, Israel B. Richardson's division, on the left bank of the creek until George Morell's division of Porter's corps could move up to replace Sumner in the tactical reserve. Morell, only one mile away at this time, marched so slowly that he did not arrive until 9:00 a.m.

By then Sumner's lead division, with its corps commander at the front, was sweeping toward the West Woods and disaster. Sedgwick's advance left William French's division behind, and those troops drifted south to encounter a hornet's nest at the Sunken Road. Sedgwick's demise, brought about by Sumner's grossly negligent reconnaissance and formation, ended the major action on the north end of the battlefield. The First and Twelfth corps had suffered appalling losses and had shot their offensive bolt for the time being. But these veterans had not stampeded. Hooker's troops held fast in the North Woods and elements of the Twelfth Corps surged around the Dunker Church until after noon. McClellan's right, though battered, could still be relied upon to stand its ground, and it had dispensed as much mayhem as it had received.

Meanwhile, French, then Richardson, raced up the furrowed fields of the Roulette Farm to the crest of a rise overlooking a narrow country lane. The Confederates here fought desperately and against great odds, but shortly after midday their defense crumbled. The center of Lee's army was now open, only a thin line of guns that Longstreet and his staff helped serve obstructing the avenue to Sharpsburg. A crisis at Antietam had been reached. Would McClellan seize the moment?

"General Lee and I knew each other well," wrote Little Mac after the war. "I had the highest respect for his ability as a commander, and knew that he was a general not to be trifled with or carelessly afforded an opportunity of striking a fatal blow.'' This image of Lee overawed McClellan's ability to evaluate battlefield realities. Rather than exploit the chance to destroy the Confederates by utilizing any of several available means, he now thought only of preventing the destruction of his own army.

Israel B. Richardson's pleas for artillery above Bloody Lane to neutralize Longstreet's guns and facilitate an infantry assault went unheeded. McClellan hoarded First Corps ordnance on the Joseph Poffenberger Farm and refused to release any of the forty-four pieces massed near the East Woods. All of these guns had but one function: to repulse a Confederate offensive against McClellan's right.

Late in the morning, several batteries crossed the Middle Bridge supported by Pleasonton's cavalry and a few infantry regiments from George Sykes's division. Shortly thereafter, these units also received orders to act strictly on the defensive. Results might be achieved by Franklin's troops, however, who began arriving from Pleasant Valley after 9:00 a.m. McClellan had not directed the Sixth Corps to rejoin the army until the evening of the sixteenth, having until then considered leaving it to operate against Maryland Heights. He persisted in this empty purpose by dispatching Darius N. Couch toward Harpers Ferry, even as Franklin's other two divisions marched toward the battlefield.

William F. ''Baldy'' Smith's brigades crossed the Antietam first, and McClellan steered them not toward Bloody Lane but to the East Woods. Prior to Smith's appearance, a daring attack by less than seven hundred Confederates under Colonel John R. Cooke had temporarily embarrassed French's right flank as it faced the Sunken Road. The Federals in turn had punished Cooke, inflicting more than 50 percent casualties. Smith's assignment, consistent with McClellan's now-dominant defensive temper, was to prevent another surprise such as Cooke had visited upon the Second Corps.

Although the tactical situation between the Mumma Farm and the West Woods had stabilized, the flashpoint having shifted to the Bloody Lane, Smith ordered William Irwin's brigade to advance toward the Dunker Church. McClellan and his defenders have ballyhooed this needless attack as a crucial turning point in the battle. Little Mac credits Smith's expedient arrival and Irwin's assault with arresting a potentially disastrous Confederate offensive. William Swinton echoes this appraisal, and Hassler avers that Smith's timely appearance ''saved the Union army from serious trouble.'' In reality, Irwin sacrificed more than two hundred New Yorkers in his isolated futility. Moreover, it is difficult to understand how McClellan and his advocates could manufacture a Confederate menace on the right. Even in the wake of Sedgwick's misadventure, the Southerners could not exploit their reclaimed momentum. Cooke's thrust had been parried with devastating results to the Rebels. With Slocum's division now on the scene, the Sixth Corps had a chance to punch through Lee's battered brigades and bring about the victory McClellan had ostensibly envisioned against Lee's left.

Longstreet's frail remnants on the Piper Farm still offered the most inviting target. McClellan's refusal to support Richardson with artillery, however, and his posting of Slocum with Smith opposite the West Woods, sidetracked any such effort. When Winfield Scott Hancock rushed to the Sunken Road to replace the fallen Richardson, he did so with orders from Little Mac merely to stand his ground. Longstreet had dodged a very large bullet.

Nevertheless, aggressive notions on the Federal side now emanated from an unlikely source. The normally cautious William Franklin pressed upon Sumner the benefits of a coordinated attack. Led by the ten thousand fresh troops of Smith and Slocum and supported by Hooker's and Mansfield's survivors, such an offensive might yet deliver a knockout blow. In a remarkable reversal of roles, Old Bull vigorously opposed Franklin's plan. The instinctively pugnacious Sumner apparently had witnessed too much carnage in the West Woods to believe that renewed assaults would succeed. Franklin disagreed vehemently with Sumner's assessment and referred the matter to the army commander. McClellan, to his credit, gave credence to his friend's proposal. He sped a courier to the front with instructions to tell the hesitant Sumner "to crowd every man and gun into ranks, and if he thinks it practicable, he may advance Franklin to carry the woods in front, holding the rest of his line with his own command, assisted by those of Banks [the Twelfth Corps] and Hooker."

McClellan thus endorsed launching an attack with less than half of his available troops on the right, two brigades of Porter's corps being sent to bolster Sumner, Hooker, Williams, and Franklin. Yet, considering the condition of Lee's left, even this fragmentary endeavor might have broken the impasse as convincingly as an assault across the Piper Farm. Sumner heard the messenger's report, but turned his back toward the Pry House with discouraging words: "Tell General McClellan I have no command. Tell him my command, Banks' command and Hooker's command are all cut-up and demoralized. Tell him General Franklin has the only organized command on this part of the field."

The courier galloped to the Pry House at 2:00 p.m., encumbered by Old Bull's wet blanket. McClellan reacted properly to this latest communiqué. He at last stirred himself from his headquarters roost and rode to the right to manage the situation in person. "Gen. Sumner expressed the most decided opinion against another attempt during the day to assault the enemy's position in front, as portions of our troops were so much scattered and demoralized," explained McClellan. "In view of these circumstances. . . I directed the different commanders to hold their positions. . . ."

Once again, the Young Napoleon stared victory in the eye and blinked. "In letting Sumner have his way here, and not insisting upon his own idea of permitting

Franklin to attack," contends Hassler, "McClellan apparently determined not to risk everything for the sake of gaining everything—it was not going to be make or break as far as he was concerned." This rationalization relies on the presumption that in the unlikely repulse of Franklin's powerful but limited attack, Lee would have retained enough potency to annihilate parts of four Union corps supported by scores of powerful and well-placed guns. The concept is simply ridiculous. McClellan's obsession with the defensive plainly squandered Franklin's uncommonly aggressive inclination. Sumner's uncharacteristic timidity, however, certainly abetted the commander's ill-fated decision.

Although Sumner is thus partially culpable for the Union's lost opportunity on September 17, another corps commander is more frequently blamed for the barren results at Antietam. Historians have accused Ambrose Burnside of every malodorous act from cowardice to treason at Sharpsburg. Those seeking the individual most responsible for Federal failure need look no farther than the commander of the Ninth Corps, according to this familiar school of thought. Burnside's "inexcusable procrastination," writes Hassler, "cost the National commander a crushing victory over Lee."

In light of the numerous errors of omission and commission wrought by McClellan, Sumner, Hooker, and other officers involved in the battle on the right, it would be patently unjust to saddle Old Burn with more than partial responsibility for the Federal frustration. In fact, while the Ninth Corps performed less than flawlessly on the south end of the field, nowhere did McClellan's unsteady hand thwart a Union victory more assuredly than on Burnside's front.

On September 16, Little Mac inspected his left flank while his engineers searched downstream from the Lower Bridge for suitable shoals along the Antietam. The staff men failed to locate highly touted Snavely's Ford, but discovered an alternative crossing less than a mile from the three-arched span. McClellan then brusquely directed Burnside to adjust his lines, exacerbating his friend's testiness arising from the army commander's unexplained detachment of Hooker's corps. Later that evening, Little Mac revisited Ninth Corps headquarters and informed his unhappy lieutenant to expect orders the next morning to negotiate the creek.

Orders did arrive at 7:00 a.m., but they merely enjoined Burnside to move forward into a position to cross the Antietam when so instructed. The ruff-whiskered Rhode Islander promptly obeyed. By 8:00 a.m. he had units assembled to storm the bridge and had directed others to push toward the ford identified by McClellan's engineers. The minutes passed. Burnside and his division commanders anxiously watched the fighting ebb and flow across distant Miller's Cornfield while Lee stripped his right to reinforce his beleaguered left. Still, the Ninth Corps sat nervously idle, waiting for the word to advance. Finally, at 10:00 a.m., Lieutenant John M. Wilson of the headquarters staff delivered the long-expected message to open the attack. McClellan's order promised to

A. Wilson Greene

Federal Assault at Burnside's Bridge

support Burnside's right, presumably with Porter's infantry and Pleasonton's cavalry, once the Ninth Corps had crossed the creek.

The tactical situation at the Lower Bridge presented a deadly challenge. Burnside recognized this and formulated a plan dependent upon three brigades wading the Antietam downstream to outflank the well-placed Confederates guarding the elevated terrain opposite the span. Unfortunately, when the Federals reached the designated ford they learned what should have been apparent to McClellan's engineers: the ripples were impracticable. A high bluff on the Union side and steep banks infested with Rebel infantry on the western shore made a crossing here too perilous to attempt. Because McClellan had not released any cavalry for reconnaissance on the left, two companies of infantry bushwhacked along the Antietam's eastern margins in search of elusive Snavely's Ford.

This offered Burnside no choice but to rush into the teeth of the Confederate resistance and attempt to carry the bridge by a coup de main. Three attempts to do so failed, but at 1:00 p.m. the 51st New York and 51st Pennsylvania charged across the stone span and drove forty weary Georgians from their rocky lairs. Two hours later, the Ninth Corps advanced again on a wide front. This time it reached the outskirts of Sharpsburg and routed the Southerners from their last line of defense. Just when victory at last seemed within grasp, A. P. Hill's division appeared following an exhausting march from Harpers Ferry. Hill's troops smashed Burnside's unprotected left flank, and the Ninth Corps stubbornly gave way, halting defiantly along the ridge above the creek. Another chance to vanquish the Army of Northern Virginia, this time by interdicting its route of retreat to Boteler's Ford on the Potomac, had slipped away.

A. P. Hill saved Lee at Sharpsburg. His Light Division shifted almost immediately from column of march into line of battle, materializing at precisely the right time in one of several potentially right places. The question on the Union left, therefore, is how might Hill's role in the battle have been obviated? Clearly, had Burnside's attack commenced earlier, even if every tactical experience remained the same, the Ninth Corps would have been in Sharpsburg while Hill's men were toiling up the Virginia shore. Jacob Cox warrants that his troops acted instantly upon receiving McClellan's attack order and that his assaults against the bridge followed one upon the other as quickly and as efficiently as possible. The culpability for not capturing the Lower Bridge until 1:00 p.m. rests less with Burnside's conduct of the operation than with McClellan's delay in unleashing it.

The Federals also might have neutralized Hill's impact by supporting the Ninth Corps advance with additional troops. This did not occur. Burnside's flanks grew more exposed with each westward step and the trauma on his left eventually rebuffed the entire Union line. Ambrose Burnside, therefore, bears no responsibility for either the tardy start or the isolated conclusion of his attacks —that responsibility lies with George McClellan.

Little Mac's misuse of the Ninth Corps stemmed from the same defensive paralysis that influenced his generalship on the right. When Hooker and Mansfield failed to destroy Lee's left in the opening maneuvers, McClellan forebore committing Burnside's troops. Not until Franklin's corps began to appear did he

Major General Ambrose Powell Hill

order Burnside forward. But the mission of the Ninth Corps had now changed drastically in McClellan's mind. No longer would Burnside support the major offensive on the right, because by midmorning McClellan had surrendered the tactical initiative. Instead, in Cox's words, Burnside's assignment became "a sort of forlorn hope to keep Lee from following up his advantages."

No wonder then that McClellan withheld his infantry reserves and all his cavalry from Burnside's afternoon attack. The Ninth Corps was to be sacrificed to prevent Lee's launching a massive counterstroke elsewhere. Of course, only A. P. Hill possessed the strength to counterattack. His brigades could have been checked, either by deploying available Union reinforcements or by employing Federal troopers to discover the Confederates before they struck.

After the battle, McClellan attempted to exonerate himself by blaming Burnside for the late start on the seventeenth. This conscious lying, repeated with distressing frequency by unwary students, reflects badly on the Young Napoleon's character. In his after-action report dated October 15, 1862, he wrote that, "Burnside's corps. . .was intrusted with the difficult task of carrying the bridge across the Antietam. . .and assaulting the enemy's right, the order having been communicated to him at 10:00 a.m."

However, on August 4, 1863, after spending nine months on the military shelf with his once-brilliant career at an ignominious end, McClellan authored a summary of his tenure as army leader. In a blatant and disingenuous attempt to rescue his reputation at the expense of his old friend, McClellan stated that he sent Burnside the directive to attack at 8:00 a.m. Only by repeated and peremptory orders, complained Little Mac, did he induce his balking subordinate to obey. He reprised this tall tale in his published memoirs. Thus by means of a self-serving fabrication did one deposed commander of the Army of the Potomac tilt responsibility for a serious error to the shoulders of another failed, and vulnerable, former commander.

At army headquarters much of the time on September 16–17, Fitz John Porter nurtured McClellan's quixotic generalship by reinforcing his commander's fantastic interpretation of battlefield verities. In an unhappy symbiosis of small-minded strategy, McClellan and Porter managed to mishandle the two divisions of the Fifth Corps on four distinct occasions. Porter amassed some nine thousand troops on the left bank of the Antietam by September 16. Posted astride the Boonsboro Turnpike opposite the Middle Bridge, the Fifth Corps served as a tactical reserve—the shock troops who, if wielded properly, might administer the coup de grace to Lee. McClellan's battle plan, in all its versions, called for an attack against the Rebel center subsequent to the success of either flanking movement. Consequently, Porter held the key to a decisive victory for the Army of the Potomac. Fitz John never turned his key in the lock. In fact, he guarded it jealously in his pocket, sustained in his prudent outlook by the army commander.

Sedgwick's calamity in the West Woods offered McClellan his first chance to drive Porter toward Sharpsburg while Lee's anemic reserves wrestled to the north. Similarly, following Sumner's assaults against the Sunken Road at a time when, according to E. P. Alexander, ''Lee's army was ruined and the end of the Confederacy was in sight,'' the route across the Middle Bridge promised Porter spectacular results. But McClellan and Porter posed at the Pry House, seeing only peril where Grant, Meade, or even Pope would have recognized opportunity.

McClellan compounded his tactical misassessment during the afternoon. Fearful about the security of his right, he ordered two of Porter's brigades to reinforce Franklin, who had himself reinforced Sumner, Williams, and Hooker. Little Mac realized during his personal examination at the front that Porter's troops were not needed in the East Woods and sent them back toward the Middle Bridge. However, in combination with his decision to detach G. K. Warren's brigade to Burnside's sector, where it accomplished nothing, McClellan managed to reduce Porter's concentrated strike force to four thousand men. Ironically, McClellan viewed this dispersal as a bold strategem, executed ''at the risk of greatly exposing our center. . . . '' Porter echoed this unfounded concern, both officers seemingly oblivious to the proximity of some eighty to one hundred cannon and Pleasonton's four thousand well-rested troopers. The belief that a body of Rebel infantry funneled toward the constricted Middle Bridge could traverse a mile of open ground and disperse eight thousand fresh soldiers and eight dozen guns speaks to McClellan's fragile hold on reality.

The static conditions on the right focused all attention upon Burnside's afternoon advance. Orlando Willcox's division on the north end of the Ninth Corps front ejected two of D. R. Jones's brigades from the fields and orchards overlooking the roads leading westward to Sharpsburg. Fifteen hundred men of Sykes's Fifth Corps division had negotiated the Middle Bridge earlier in the day, but provided scant assistance to Willcox's assault. Now, however, the Boonsboro Pike lay unobstructed all the way to the streets of the village, which rapidly filled with routed Confederates. One of Sykes's field officers sent a courier to division headquarters requesting permission to exploit this confusion. Captain Thomas M. Anderson of the 9th U.S. Infantry watched as Sykes, Porter, and McClellan pondered the proposition. ''We received no orders to advance,'' reported the captain, ''although the advance of a single brigade. . .would have cut Lee's army in two.'' After the war, Sykes told Anderson that ''he thought McClellan was inclined to order in the Fifth Corps, but when he spoke of doing so Fitz John Porter said: 'Remember, General! I command the last reserve of the last Army of the Republic.' ''

Shortly afterward, as A. P. Hill drove the Ninth Corps toward Antietam Creek, McClellan looked beseechingly at Porter, who stood by his commander's side scanning the field to his left. Porter turned, faced the general, and slowly shook

Major General Fitz John Porter

his head. Little Mac then replied to Burnside's pleas for help: "I will send...Miller's battery. I can do nothing more. I have no infantry."

Burnside maintained his position above the bridge, but his two attacks and ultimate repulse cost him more than twenty-three hundred casualties. Porter lost barely one hundred men all day. Like Sumner before him, the Fifth Corps commander failed utterly to possess the imagination necessary to win the engagement. Unlike Sumner, Porter's intimacy with McClellan ensured that the latter would heed his lieutenant's fainthearted advice.

Little Mac's willingness to accede to the tremulous counsel of Sumner and Porter is merely symptomatic of his reluctance to exercise any degree of tactical control over the battle. His one appearance on the field did generate the usual enthusiasm, and had McClellan wished to galvanize his popularity into action, the demoralization he decried would have dissipated. But leadership by personal example, a quality displayed by every great captain, eluded George McClellan. The Army of the Potomac, from corps command through the ranks, fought at Antietam without a single guiding hand, and paid a heavy bounty in blood and frustration.

Darkness brought a cessation of hostilities but not an end to the suffering. As the pitiable cries of the wounded rent the night, the Union high command experienced the mental agony of momentous decision. Albert D. Richardson of the *New York Tribune* overheard McClellan remark that, "We must fight tonight and tomorrow. If we succeed we end the war." If the reporter's ears could be believed, Little Mac had undergone a miraculous metamorphosis. The night passed quietly, however, and as the sun rose over South Mountain, the immobile armies glared at one another across the corpse-strewn fields they had contested the day before.

McClellan telegraphed both his wife and General Halleck with the news of the terrible engagement and with predictions for further combat. "The battle will probably be renewed today," read Old Brains. "Send all the troops you can by the most expeditious route." Ellen learned that the fight on the seventeenth "was a success, but whether a decided victory depends on what occurs today." Little Mac neglected to mention, however, that any fighting on September 18 would be initiated by Lee. "A careful and anxious survey of the condition of my command, and my knowledge of the enemy's forces and position," temporized the general in his preliminary report, "failed to impress me with any reasonable certainty of success if I renewed the attack without reinforcing columns."

McClellan built upon this theme in his memoirs and final report. "At this critical juncture I should have had a narrow view of the condition of the country had I been willing to hazard another battle with less than absolute assurance of success. . . . One battle lost, and almost all would have been lost. Lee's army might then have marched as it pleased on Washington, Baltimore, Philadelphia, or New York." The soldiers suffered from fatigue and hunger, explained Little Mac, and the artillery lacked ammunition. Meade, Williams, Sumner, and Burnside presided over allegedly demoralized troops, and combat-ready reinforcements were not available until later in the day. Moreover, most of the army's senior commanders, particularly Sumner, recommended against an offensive.

Had all of this—indeed, any significant part of it—been true, McClellan's decision not to risk battle might have been justified. Unfortunately, he constructed his after-the-fact rationale on a flimsy foundation of poor judgment, weak generalship, and prevarication. He cited "long day and night marches" as a source of exhaustion for his army, activities experienced by few Federal brigades. The Fifth and Sixth corps between them counted more than twenty thousand fresh muskets, and the First, Twelfth, and Ninth corps enjoyed better spirits and greater numbers than McClellan reported. Furthermore, two new divisions arrived in the morning, Couch's and A. A. Humphreys's, adding twelve thousand effectives to the equation. Little Mac grossly misrepresented Humphreys's service-ability, an injustice that the division commander angrily challenged. All told, some sixty-two thousand Federals stood poised to resume the battle before noon on September 18.

Lee counted about half that number of all arms and in all degrees of hunger, fatigue, and demoralization. The Army of Northern Virginia hunkered far from its base, in hostile territory, with an obstacle in its rear. The seizure of Nicodemus Heights, an operation advocated by William Franklin, would have imperiled the entire Southern line. But Little Mac allowed the critical moment to pass. This was a time, said journalist Richardson, "when by daring something, the destiny of the nation might have been changed. . . ." One of Porter's men vented his frustration in a letter home: "Why in the name of heaven McClellan did not renew the battle on Thursday, and follow speedily across the river, I can't understand. . . . I am provoked, perhaps without cause, but I cannot help feeling that it prolongs this horrid war."

McClellan professed his intention to attack on September 19, but save for a message telling Franklin to be prepared to advance, no evidence exists to corroborate the claim. Lee withdrew during the night, and the Young Napoleon permitted him to escape. "To us of the Thirteenth Massachusetts, it seemed just possible that the enemy might be equally tired and a good deal more dis-comfited," lamented one soldier, but the Confederate army negotiated the Potomac without the loss of a single wagon or gun. The commanding general wired Halleck at 8:30 a.m. with word of Lee's departure: "Last night the enemy abandoned his position, leaving his dead and wounded on the field. We are again in pursuit. I do not yet know whether he is falling back to an interior position or crossing the river. We may safely claim a complete victory."

Did McClellan really believe that his army's cautious probing constituted "pursuit"? Probably not. He realized that bold words played well in Washington and willingly provided the desired rhetoric.

Did McClellan really believe that forcing Lee back to Virginia constituted a "complete victory"? Undoubtedly so. In fact, this perception explains McClellan's conduct of the entire Maryland campaign. At 10:30 a.m. on September 19, McClellan informed the general-in-chief that Lee had crossed the Potomac. He then refined his definition of the consummate conquest. "The enemy is driven back into Virginia. Maryland and Pennsylvania are now safe.'' The following day, McClellan wrote his wife that, ''Our victory was complete, and the disorganized rebel army had rapidly returned to Virginia, its dreams of 'invading Pennsylvania' dissipated forever. I feel some little pride in having, with a beaten and demoralized army, defeated Lee so utterly and saved the North so completely.'' Forty-eight hours later he announced that, ''I look upon this campaign as substantially ended, and my present intention is. . .to work and reorganize the army. . . .''

Accepting George McClellan's postwar writing at face value usually invites problems. In regard to his perspective on the objectives on the Maryland campaign, however, his memoirs are credible:

> Had Gen. Lee remained in front of Washington it would have been the part of wisdom to hold our own army quiet until its pressing wants were fully supplied, its organization restored, and its ranks filled with recruits. . . . But as the enemy maintained the offensive. . .it became necessary to meet him at any cost. . .and throw him back across the Potomac. . . . It must be borne constantly in mind that the purpose of advancing from Washington was simply to meet the necessities of the moment by frustrating Lee's invasion of the Northern States, and, when that was accomplished, to push with the utmost rapidity the work of reorganization and supply. . . .

Major John J. Key of Halleck's staff, brother of Colonel Thomas Key of McClellan's staff, told an officer in Washington after the battle that Little Mac intentionally allowed Lee's army to escape destruction. ''That is not the game,'' whispered Key. ''The object is that neither army shall get much advantage of the other; that both shall be kept in the field till they are exhausted, when we will make a compromise and save slavery.'' Did McClellan actually participate in such a traitorous plot? Probably not, although it is equally preposterous to pretend, as do some of McClellan's biographers, that he possessed the prescience to know that merely thwarting Lee's incursion would extinguish Confederate hopes to change the complexion of the war through British recognition and intervention.

The battle of Antietam did alter the nature of the Civil War, but it did so in spite, not because, of George McClellan. Visions of a limited war, a compromise peace, and a return to the old order of national affairs lay dying beside twenty-three thousand American casualties in Washington County. As a model for analyzing the military capacity of George Brinton McClellan, however, the Maryland campaign is most instructive. McClellan was an organizer, not a field commander, and by the autumn of 1862 the Army of the Potomac needed a fighter, not a facilitator. McClellan ''had the pendantry of war rather than the inspiration of war,'' writes William Swinton. ''His talent was eminently that of the cabinet; and his proper place was in Washington, where he should have remained as general-in-chief. . . ."

In addition to his deficiencies as a tactician, McClellan's generalship suffered from self-deception. As T. Harry Williams says, McClellan lacked "a sense of realism. Almost literally he lived in a world of make-believe. . . ." His appraisals of Lee's strength, the elasticity of his own men, and the outcome of the campaign all demonstrate his fragile grip on the facts. Little Mac's unshakable confidence in the efficacy of an overwhelming mobilization that would render Confederate resistance patently useless evinced an absolute failure to appreciate political considerations in a democratic war. Stephen Sears identifies a "messianic vision" in McClellan that convinced the general that he was God's chosen instrument and therefore impervious to criticism. Consequently, advice that did not coincide with the Young Napoleon's personal persuasions fell on deaf ears.

Robert E. Lee took the measure of his counterpart in Marlyand and based his strategy around it. A. L. Long states that Lee "availed himself of McClellan's over-caution and essayed perilous movements which he could not have ventured in the presence of a more active opponent." Lee himself attested to this evaluation. When informed of McClellan's removal in November 1862, he remarked to Longstreet, "I fear they may continue to make these changes till they find someone whom I don't understand."

That process would take time, as would the transition from McClellan's brand of warfare to the modern methods of Grant, Sherman, and Sheridan. Those three soldiers might never have emerged from the obscurity of the West, however, had the Federal commander in Maryland been equal to a unique challenge. Between September 13 and 18, 1862, George McClellan discarded the best opportunity ever offered to destroy the Confederacy's principal field army. The nation met the price of his failure during thirty-one additional months of Civil War.

GARY W. GALLAGHER

The Maryland Campaign
in Perspective

The broad consequences of the 1862 Maryland campaign exceeded those of any other operation of the American Civil War. The events of that autumn marked a watershed in the conflict. Soldiers and civilians alike strove to discover exactly what had been won and lost in a military sense. People behind the lines struggled to come to terms with hideous casualty lists. Photographic evidence from the battlefield at Antietam altered forever romantic conceptions of war. Abraham Lincoln took a momentous step toward emancipation, while European leaders recast their thinking about the likelihood of Confederate independence. Maryland remained firmly in the Union; Republicans breathed a bit more easily about the coming Northern elections. Complex in execution and impact, the Maryland campaign qualified as a pivotal event of the war.

In the area of military results, only the magnitude and horror of the fighting were beyond conflicting interpretation. A Pennsylvania soldier groping for the right words to describe the carnage stated simply, "No tongue can tell, no mind conceive, no pen portray the horrible sights I witnessed this morning." "Great God," wrote a Georgian to his wife the day after the battle, "what awful things I have to chronicle this morning!. . .One of the most awful battles that was ever fought was fought yesterday[.] [It] commenced at daylight and continued all day until dark. . . . This war will have to stop before long, as all the men will be killed off." Similar statements from other men appalled by the savagery of the battle abound in the literature on Antietam.

The overall military result of the campaign was more open to question. Almost from the moment the guns fell silent in the gathering dusk of September 17, 1862, people expressed contradictory reactions about what had transpired. Lee's official report and congratulatory order to his troops understandably emphasized the positive aspects of the expedition. The Confederate army had cleared Federals from northern Virginia, captured Harpers Ferry and its garrison, provisioned itself from western Maryland, and maintained a position near the south bank of the Potomac after its withdrawal. As for his soldiers' conduct in the battle, Lee told Davis with obvious pride that, "History records but few examples of a greater amount of labor and fighting than has been done by this army during the present campaign." To the Army of Northern Virginia, Lee expressed "'admiration of the indomitable courage it has displayed in battle and its cheerful endurance of privation and hardship on the march." Absent was any hint of the straggling and desertion that had plagued Lee's movements; however, in a letter to Davis on September 25 Lee admitted that the army did not "exhibit its former temper and condition." James Longstreet, who doubtless was privy to Lee's thinking in the aftermath of the raid, recorded after the war that "General Lee was not satisfied with the result of the Maryland campaign."

Opinion from the Southern ranks generally spoke of success. Letters, diaries, and postwar accounts mentioned the prisoners and guns taken at Harpers Ferry, the steadfast courage of the men at Antietam, and McClellan's failure to drive the Army of Northern Virginia from the battlefield on September 18. "At night we lay down on our arms," remembered a Virginian of the night of September 17. "The next morning, expecting a renewal of the battle, we were up bright and early. But the enemy was badly whipped and did not make a demonstration during the day." Chaplain Nicholas A. Davis of Hood's Texas Brigade stated shortly after the campaign that "Harper's Ferry had fallen, and its rich prizes were ours." Davis emphasized that "our march to and across the river was undisturbed—This, of itself, will show to the world the nature of McClellan's victory. And if he had beaten and driven us,...why did he allow us to pass quietly away after holding the field a whole day and night?"

John Hampden Chamberlayne, a Virginia artillerist, cautioned his sister not "to suppose we were driven out of Maryland; no such thing; our campaign is almost unexampled for quickness & completeness of success." "We have done much more," Chamberlayne insisted, "than a sane man could have expected." In *The Lost Cause*, published in 1866, Edward A. Pollard suggested that the campaign had "few parallels in history for active operations and brilliant results." Pollard noted sarcastically that if "McClellan was under the impression that he had won a victory, he showed but little disposition to improve it, or to gather its fruits."

Confederate General Jubal A. Early ably enumerated the positive facets of the Maryland raid in his postwar autobiography. After forcing Union armies away from Richmond and out of northern Virginia, Lee "had crossed the Potomac, captured an important stronghold defended by a strong force, securing a large amount of artillery, small arms, and stores of all kinds. . . . " At Antietam he "fought a great battle with the newly reorganized and heavily reinforced and recruited army of the enemy, which later was so badly crippled that it was not able to resume the offensive for nearly two months." Lee then stood "defiantly on the banks of the Potomac, the extreme northern limit of the Confederacy," and from that position menaced Washington while at the same time freeing Richmond from direct threat. When the Federals finally moved into Virginia again, stated Early, Lee was in perfect position "to interpose his army, and inflict a new defeat on the enemy."

A few Confederates confessed doubts about their accomplishments in Maryland. Four days after Antietam, Walter H. Taylor of Lee's staff somewhat bitterly counseled his sister not to "let any of your friends sing 'My Maryland'— not 'my Western Maryland' anyhow." "We do not claim a victory. . . ," conceded Taylor, "It was not decisive enough for that." The young staff officer did add bravely that if either side had an edge at Antietam, "it certainly was with us." Brigadier General William Dorsey Pender informed his wife Fanny that he had heard but one feeling expressed about the raid into Maryland, "and that is a regret at our having gone there. Our Army has shown itself incapable of invasion and we had better stick to the defensive." A member of the Rockbridge Artillery made no effort to soften his blunt assessment: "The yankees slitely got the best of the fight in Maryland. You ought to have Seen us Skeedadling across the Potomac and the yankees close in our rear." South Carolinian Alexander Cheves Haskell praised the fighting qualities of the Confederates at Antietam, but stressed that huge numbers of their comrades had abandoned the army. "We are in far better condition in every respect," he affirmed from the Virginia side of the Potomac on September 28, "than when we first invaded the cold, treacherous soil of Maryland."

Voices on the Federal side also reflected mixed judgments about the military results of the campaign. Politics and personal loyalty colored many Northern attitudes—friends and supporters of the Democratic McClellan in one camp, Republicans and McClellan's enemies within the Union army arrayed against them. McClellan himself stood at one extreme, a pillar of unrelenting self-congratulation. He took pains to impress Mrs. McClellan with the magnitude of his achievement: "I feel some little pride in having, with a beaten and demoralized army, defeated Lee so utterly and saved the North so completely." "I have the satisfaction of knowing," he continued, "that God has, in His mercy, a second time made me the instrument for saving the nation." General-in-Chief Henry W. Halleck received, on September 19, McClellan's bombastic assurance that "our victory was complete. The enemy is driven back into Virginia. Maryland and Pennsylvania are now safe." Neither at the time nor in his postwar writings did McClellan grant that his conduct of the campaign had been anything less than brilliant.

For many Northerners, the fact of Lee's retreat signified a Union victory. Alpheus S. Williams, a divisional leader in the Federal Twelfth Corps, believed that "we punished the Rebels severely in the last battle. The number of dead they left on the field was enormous. In some places whole regiments seem to have fallen in their tracks." The Confederates sneaked back to Virginia, said

Williams: "Their invasion of Maryland has been a sad business for them." George G. Meade, who as commander of the Army of the Potomac would repel a second Confederate raid nine months hence, pronounced Lee's Maryland adventure "the most lamentable failure." Although his unit did not fight at Antietam, Colonel Robert McAllister of the 11th New Jersey sent a letter to his family on September 21 that echoed McClellan's own estimate of the campaign: "McClellan has done well—gained a decided victory, saved Washington, Maryland, and Pennsylvania, and given the Rebels a hard stroke." "How splendidly his men fought under him, compared to what the troops did under Pope," McAllister added. Edward K. Wightman of the 9th New York arrived on the battlefield just after the Army of Northern Virginia had retreated. "The impression among our soliders," he found, "is that the war is finished. They think the battle of Wednesday the greatest of the war and decisive." A young officer from Massachusetts who heard the gunfire from Antietam but missed the battle recalled that it "was claimed as a victory by the Army of the Potomac because they held the field."

Some Federals sensed that McClellan had frittered away a splendid opportunity. Robert Goldthwaite Carter of Massachusetts and his three brothers, whose letters form a wonderful chronicle of the war in the East, considered Antietam at best a partial victory. One of the Carters had difficulty understanding why "McClellan did not let our corps finish up the 'rebs,' " and especially why the Federal commander allowed Lee to stand along Antietam Creek undisturbed throughout September 18 and then to cross the Potomac safely. Another brother also lamented the fact that the Confederates got away "to our shame, without much loss to their rear guard." "If McClellan had only attacked again early Thursday morning," observed disappointed Northern newspaper correspondent Albert D. Richardson two days after Antietam, "we could have driven them into the river or captured them. . . . It was one of the supreme moments when by daring something, the destiny of the nation might have been changed." Union First Corps chief Joseph Hooker agreed. An officer who visited the wounded general in Keedysville on September 19 recorded that he "talked a great deal about McClellan not renewing the attack yesterday."

No one in the North experienced deeper disappointment than Abraham Lincoln. He had considered Lee's movement into Maryland a wonderful opening for a Federal counterstroke. Far from home and tied to the fords on the Potomac, Lee was vulnerable to determined pressure. Antietam made a good start on the business of finishing Lee, but McClellan's inactivity on September 18 allowed the Confederate chieftain to extricate his army from a dangerous position. Lincoln prodded and implored McClellan to move, until finally, when seven weeks had passed and Lee remained ensconced in the northern frontier of Virginia, Lincoln removed Little Mac from command. A reading of Lincoln's correspondence with McClellan in that seven weeks conveys the depth of his disappointment and frustration. So too does Gideon Welles's entry in his diary for September 19, 1862: "Nothing from the army, except that, instead of following up the victory, attacking and capturing the Rebels, they, after a day's armistice, are rapidly escaping across the river." And then, in exasperation, the dour secretary of the navy went on, "McClellan says they are crossing, and that Pleasonton is after them. Oh dear!"

What is a fair reckoning of the military ledger sheet of the 1862 Maryland campaign? The Confederate side is a fascinating blend of accomplishment and useless loss, of brilliant leadership on the battlefield and questionable strategic decisions after September 15. Lee's movement north represented an effort to take the war out of Virginia, gather food and fodder, threaten Washington from the west, and prevent another Union incursion south of the Potomac before the onset of winter. He accomplished the first three of these, and managed also to postpone the next Federal drive toward Richmond until Ambrose E. Burnside's unusual winter campaign that ended ignominiously for the Union at Fredericksburg in mid-December. Mounting a raid rather than an invasion, Lee knew he would have to fall back to Virginia at some point, preferably in late fall. The battle of Antietam compelled him to withdraw sooner than he wished. But because McClellan allowed him to maintain a position immediately south of the Potomac, Lee was able to accomplish from northern Virginia what he had planned to do in western Maryland or southern Pennsylvania. The captures at Harpers Ferry constituted a bonus that Lee did not envision at the outset.

Against these positive results must be reckoned the loss of more than a quarter of the Army of Northern Virginia. The vast majority of those casualties came at Antietam, where Lee stood to gain not a single military advantage. After the fighting on South Mountain, Lee retained no viable offensive options. Harpers Ferry had fallen. No hope of surprise remained; an overwhelmingly more powerful foe was closing in from the east. The astute Porter Alexander subsequently observed that on September 15 "our whole army was back on the Va. side of the Potomac except Longstreet's & Hill's divisions. These could have been easily retired across the river, & we would, indeed, have left Maryland without a great battle, but we would nevertheless have come off with good prestige & a very fair lot of prisoners & guns, & lucky on the whole to do this, considering the accident of the 'lost order.' " Lee erred badly in choosing to give battle at Sharpsburg it was, thought Alexander, his "greatest military blunder." His back was against the river, only Boteler's Ford invited escape should a crisis arise, and the disparity in numbers virtually guaranteed that the army would face a bitter contest.

Ironically, this battle that Lee should not have fought proved a showcase for the Confederate high command. Lee, Jackson, and Longstreet directed a tactical masterpiece, and their soldiers added heroic luster to a reputation already high.

They also fell in such numbers that the Confederate government in Richmond hesitated to publish casualty lists for fear of the effect on the home front.

While fighting at Antietam was a mistake, Lee's decision to stay on the field another day and contemplate a counterattack amounted to sheer folly. The usual explanations are well known: Lee wanted the men to stand their ground lest morale drop; Lee knew the cautious McClellan would risk no further assaults; or, Lee felt confident of his army's ability to repulse the enemy. These rationalizations wither under even the slightest scrutiny. Lee realized all too well that morale already sagged among thousands of his soldiers. How would potentially catastrophic defeat along the river improve it? The second argument is equally flimsy. McClellan had attacked for twelve hours on September 17. How could Lee possibly know he would fail to resume those efforts on the eighteenth? As for the contention that Lee's army could repulse the enemy, the seventeenth had been a series of near disasters for Lee, and no factor had changed in his favor. Another round of similar assaults on September 18 almost certainly would break his army. In *R. E. Lee: A Biography,* Douglas Southall Freeman steps back in awe of Lee's resolute stand on the eighteenth: "What manner of man was he who would elect after that doubtful battle against vast odds to stand for another day with his back to the river?" The answer is that the R. E. Lee of September 18, 1862, was a man who irresponsibly placed at peril his entire army.

If Lee's gravest error was in striving to do too much with a limited force, McClellan's was in asking too little of a powerful one. High marks must be his for restoring confidence and discipline to a recently defeated army. He also forced Lee out of Maryland, a principal Federal goal in the campaign. In his mind that may have been enough. McClellan wanted a restoration of the old Union with the least possible cost in blood. He may have thought Antietam impressive enough to convince Southerners that independence was beyond their grasp, whereas a more decisive triumph might provide a springboard for Republicans to solidify their political grip on the nation and construct a new Union without slavery.

The salient feature of the entire Maryland campaign, however, was McClellan's opportunity to inflict a catastrophic defeat on Lee's army. No other commander on either side during the Civil War enjoyed a comparable situation. Following receipt of Lee's Special Orders No. 191, McClellan dawdled while the Army of Northern Virginia lay scattered across western Maryland. On September 15–16 he allowed Lee to concentrate his far-flung units near Sharpsburg. Porter Alexander's critique of McClellan at Antietam conveys a proper sense of disbelief: Lee managed a tactical draw on that day only "by the Good Lord's putting it into McClellan's heart to keep Fitz John Porter's corps entirely out to the battle, & Franklin's nearly all out." "I doubt whether many hearts but McClellan's would have accepted the suggestions, even from a Divine source," noted

Alexander wryly. "For Common Sense was just shouting, 'Your adversary is backed against a river, with no bridge & only one ford, & that the worst one on the whole river. If you whip him now you destroy him utterly, root & branch & bag & baggage. . . . & such game is worth great risks. Every man must fight & keep on fighting for all he is worth.' " "No military genius," concluded Alexander, "but only the commonest kind of every day common sense, was necessary to appreciate that."

Priceless openings had come and gone over three crucial days, and Lee's decision to hold his lines on September 18 was McClellan's ultimate opportunity. Reinforced during the night, he outnumbered Lee nearly three to one. Thousands of his men were fresh, the enemy fatigued beyond telling. But once again McClellan lacked the fortitude to let his loyal soldiers seek complete victory. For all the talk of McClellan's love for his men, one fact stands out—he doubted their ability to defeat Lee's veterans. Their valor the day before on the rolling hills west of Antietam Creek fully matched that of the Confederate defenders. Their numbers should have told then; they would have told on September 18. They waited and watched through a long, tense day, and then it was over. The Army of Northern Virginia marched away that night to execute an undisputed crossing at Boteler's Ford. The Army of the Potomac possessed the requisite elements to deliver a fatal blow. Destruction of Lee's army would have uncovered Richmond and crippled Southern morale; it might have ended the war. Because McClellan chose not to force the issue, his military performance in Maryland must be judged harshly.

The absence of a clear-cut military decision in Maryland both bewildered and discouraged civilians in the North and South. Lee had hoped a successful raid would lead Northerners to examine the utility of continuing the war. But while his brief sojourn in Maryland prompted renewed scrutiny of Northern military leadership, it triggered no groundswell of support for a negotiated peace leading to Confederate independence. Many Northerners adopted an attitude similar to that of Republican war correspondent Whitelaw Reid, who pointed out that while the Confederates "certainly did not entirely succeed, if *we* claim the success, they can retort with force that never was victory more dear or barren." "Nor can any charity explain away that terrible, fateful delay after claiming a glorious victory," continued Reid. "It will not do to say our men were exhausted. If the vanquished and dispirited army had strength enough to gather up its fragments and retreat, the victorious army must have had strength enough to follow." "Let no weary patriot be deceived," Reid warned in summary. "We, indeed, took no steps backward at Antietam Creek, but we took very few forward."

Civilian sentiment south of the Potomac was generally pessimistic. Robert Garlick Hill Kean of the Confederate Bureau of War characterized Jefferson Davis in his diary as being "very low down after the battle of Sharpsburg."

Davis confessed to Secretary of War George Wythe Randolph that the Confederacy's "maximum strength had been laid out, while the enemy was but beginning to put forth his." A young woman in Front Royal, Virginia, recorded with apprehension that "reports concerning the Sharpsburg battle are confirmed...our army are certainly recrossing the river. It looks rather gloomy for our prospects in Md. and I cannot possibly understand it all." The government did not at first disclose official figures for casualties — "a bad sign for us," thought Catherine Edmondston of Halifax County, North Carolina. "The possession of Harpers Ferry was claimed by us as worth the advance into Maryland," wrote Edmondston, "& yet we cannot hold it. God be with us! Turn not away Thy face, O God, but be with our army a help in time of need." Despite early stories in the *Richmond Enquirer* and elsewhere that Antietam was a stunning Confederate victory, few Southerners believed for long that the Maryland campaign had been more than a bloody standoff at best.

For Northerners, Antietam signaled a special turning point in the war. Photographers reached the battlefield before the dead had been buried—a first in American history. Their probing cameras captured the horrors along the Hagerstown Pike, east of the Dunker Church, and in the ghastly Sunken Road. In October 1862, Mathew Brady's New York gallery placed on exhibit a series of views entitled "The Dead at Antietam." Long lines of people passed through the gallery, including a reporter for the *New York Times* who described the experience in an article published on October 20. "Mr. Brady has done something to bring home to us the terrible reality and earnestness of war," he wrote. "If he has not brought the bodies and laid them in our door-yards and along the streets, he had done something very like it. . . . " *Harper's Weekly* and *Atlantic Monthly* also carried stories about the photographs, and *Harper's* included woodcuts of some of the death studies. Profoundly moved, those who saw the pictures would never again think of battle as carefully dressed ranks of brave men moving gallantly forward. Their understanding of war now included images of the twisted bodies of North Carolinians and Louisianians, of dead horses and broken equipment, and of a blasted landscape.

Apart from the debatable issue of military success, Lee's raid into Maryland was a profound failure. The most telling consequence came on September 22, 1862, when Lincoln told his cabinet that he would issue a preliminary proclamation of emancipation. Lincoln conceded that "the action of the army against the rebels has not been quite what I should have best liked. But they have been driven out of Maryland, and Pennsylvania is no longer in danger of invasion." That was victory enough to spare the proclamation any tinge of desperation. Should the states in rebellion refuse to return to the Union by January 1, 1863, said the president, their chattels "shall be then, thenceforward, and forever free." Vigorous and sometimes ugly debate ensued across the North, where millions of whites who hated or feared blacks resisted the notion of fighting in part to cast off the slaves' shackles. The South reacted with violent scorn, pointing out that Lincoln was freeing slaves only where he lacked the power to do so. What he really wanted, Southerners argued, was to precipitate a race war in the Confederacy. Lincoln's exemption of loyal Border States and all areas of the Confederacy under Federal control as of January 1, 1863, also led a few abolitionists in the North and Europe to charge hypocrisy. A number of twentieth-century historians have raised the same cry.

These critics displayed a poor grasp of the proclamation. Lincoln saw it as a war measure aimed at hastening Confederate defeat. Under the Constitution, he could seize material from the rebellious Confederacy; however, he lacked authority to take personal property from citizens residing in areas loyal to the United States government. He had done what was possible, and thereby helped open the way for nearly two hundred thousand black men to fight in Federal armies. The proclamation also foreclosed the option of reunion on the basis of the status quo ante bellum. The South's social and economic structure was doomed unless Confederate armies won independence on the battlefield. With issuance of the proclamation, the struggle became a total war for Union and freedom.

Lee's retreat from Maryland and the Emancipation Proclamation both influenced events in Europe. At flood tide in early September, Southern hopes for help from Europe receded quickly. Prime Minister Palmerston believed that "these last battles in Maryland have rather set the North up again." "The whole matter is full of difficulty," he thought, "and can only be cleared up by some more decided events between the contending armies." In a letter to Lord Russell on October 2, Palmerston suggested that "ten days or a fortnight more may throw a clearer light upon future prospects." William Gladstone and Russell continued their agitation for recognition through October. On the seventh of that month, Gladstone delivered his memorable paean to the Confederacy in a speech at Tyneside: "Jefferson Davis and other leaders of the South have made an army; they are making, it appears, a navy; and they have made what is more than either, they have made a nation."

The loud cheers that greeted those strident phrases were long forgotten when the British cabinet took up the question of recognition on October 28, 1862. With Palmerston made cautious by Antietam, the vote went against Russell and Gladstone. Shortly thereafter the cabinet also refused a French plan calling for Britain, France, and Russia to suggest a six-month armistice and suspension of the blockade. News of the Emancipation Proclamation further undercut friends of the South. American Minister to England Charles Francis Adams wrote happily that British antislavery sentiment was working to "annihilate all agitation for recognition." Adams undoubtedly overstated the impact of Lincoln's proclamation, for even some abolitionists in England continued to support the Confederacy.

Neither Lee's withdrawal from Maryland nor the proclamation guaranteed that Europe would stay aloof, but together they helped persuade the British to wait until military developments favored the Confederates. Southern arms ultimately proved unequal to the daunting task of compiling enough victories to bring European intercession.

Lee's expectation of gathering recruits in Maryland came to little. Indeed, Southern illusions about pro-Confederate Marylanders waiting to break free of Union oppression disappeared even before the battle of Antietam. As early as September 7, Lee cautioned Davis that "notwithstanding individual expressions of kindness that have been given," he did not "anticipate any general rising of the people in our behalf." The next day, September 8, Lee issued a proclamation informing Marylanders that "our army has come among you, and is prepared to assist you with the power of its arms in regaining the rights of which you have been despoiled." No more than a few hundred Marylanders stepped forward to join the thin ranks of the Army of Northern Virginia.

The numerous Germans in western Maryland turned a distinctly cold shoulder to the intruders. The ragged clothing and gaunt frames of the Confederates, as well as their lice and pungent odor, put off even sympathetic civilians. In Frederick, citizens joyously welcomed McClellan's troops after the Army of Northern Virginia had moved on to the west. "Happy homelike faces beamed on us. . . ," wrote a Massachusetts soldier of his arrival in Frederick, "the people began to cook for us, bringing out as we passed, cake, pie and bread." A New Yorker related that "the place was alive with girls going around the streets in squads waving flags, singing songs & inviting the soldiers in for hot suppers."

As the Southern army crossed the Potomac into Virginia on the night of September 18, John H. Lewis of the 9th Virginia Infantry noted a changed attitude toward Maryland: "When going over the river the boys were singing 'Maryland, my Maryland.' But all was quiet on that point when we came back. Occasionally some fellow would strike that tune, and you would then hear the echo, 'Damn My Maryland.' All seemed to be disgusted with that part of Maryland."

Lee experienced a final failure relating to the Northern elections that fall. He had hoped to strengthen the peace interests, but the Army of Northern Virginia's two-week stay north of the Potomac supplied poor aid to those who opposed the Republican administration. If Union half-victories at Antietam and Perryville spawned little if any rejoicing in the North, they at least avoided the sort of dramatic defeat that might have sent Republican fortunes spinning downward. Ironically, the Emancipation Proclamation—made possible by Lee's retreat— did provoke angry reaction that helped the Democrats. Results of the canvass of 1862 showed only modest Democratic gains for an off-year election—thirty-four seats in the House of Representatives, gubernatorial victories in New York and New Jersey, and control of the Illinois and Indiana legislatures. The

Republicans managed to gain five seats in the Senate and retain control of the House (their net loss in the House was the smallest in the last ten elections for the majority party). The war would continue under Republican direction.

The Maryland campaign holds a unique position in the galaxy of Civil War military operations. Its centerpiece was the surging maelstrom of Antietam, which stood out as the bloodiest single day of a conflict marked by great slaughter. The principal commanders offered a striking contrast in personality and style—Lee pressing his worn army to the edge of ruin in pursuit of beckoning opportunity; McClellan repeatedly shrinking from commitment of his proud host in circumstances favorable beyond the imaginings of most generals. Etched in grays rather than black and white, the military resolution invited debate. Lee went north and fought, avoided a series of lurking disasters, and found refuge in the end along the southern bank of the Potomac River. But the military events of mid-September 1862 bore bitter political and diplomatic fruit for the Confederacy. The nature of the conflict changed because of Lee's Maryland campaign. The South might have won the old war—seemed in the giddy season of late summer and fall 1862 to be doing so. But the new war would admit of no easy reconciliation because the stakes had been raised to encompass the entire social fabric of the South. The war after Antietam would demand a decisive resolution on the battlefield, and that the Confederacy could not achieve.

Bibliographic Note

There is a large and diverse literature on the 1862 Maryland campaign. Any military analysis must begin with the U.S. War Department's *The War of the Rebellion: A Compilation of the Official Records of the Union and Confederate Armies* (127 vols., index, and atlas; Washington, D.C., 1880–1901). Reports, orders, and correspondence relating to Antietam fill the two large books of series I, volume 19, parts 1 and 2, of the *Official Records* (or the *OR,* as the set is popularly known), and more than any other single source this material helps to define the scope and progress of the campaign. A number of participants contributed useful, though frequently self-serving, articles to the Century Company's four-volume *Battles and Leaders of the Civil War* (ed. Clarence Clough Buel and Robert Underwood Johnson; New York, 1887). Pieces on the Maryland campaign by George B. McClellan, D. H. Hill, Jacob D. Cox, William B. Franklin, James Longstreet, and other Northern and Southern commanders appear in volume 2.

Diaries, reminiscences, collections of letters, and other works by officers and men in the ranks run into the hundreds and vary widely in quality. *The Wartime Papers of R. E. Lee* (ed. Clifford Dowdey and Louis H. Manarin; Boston, 1961) and *The Civil War Papers of George B. McClellan: Selected Correspondence 1860–1865* (ed. Stephen W. Sears; New York, 1989) reveal the thinking of the two principal commanders. Although often untrustworthy, *McClellan's Own Story* (New York, 1887), the general's posthumous memoir, is a must on the campaign. E. P. Alexander's *Military Memoirs of a Confederate* (New York, 1907) and *Fighting for the Confederacy* (Chapel Hill, N.C., 1989), attest to their author's remarkable ability to get at the essence of an operation. A careful treatment by Stonewall Jackson's chief of ordnance is William Allan's *The Army of Northern Virginia in 1862* (Boston, 1892). James Longstreet's *From Manassas to Appomattox* (Philadelphia, 1896) makes available material on the Confederate side to be found nowhere else. Four unusually good Federal accounts are Alpheus S. Williams's often gripping *From the Cannon's Mouth* (ed. Milo M. Quaife; Detroit, 1959), Francis W. Palfrey's general examination of the war in the East during the fall and winter of 1862 titled *The Antietam and Fredericksburg* (New York, 1882), Robert Goldthwaite Carter's remarkable family chronicle *Four Brothers in Blue* (reprint of the scarce original edition; Austin, Tex., 1978), and Charles S. Wainwright's superlative wartime letters published as

A Diary of Battle (ed. Allan Nevins; New York, 1962). Henry Kyd Douglas's *I Rode with Stonewall* (Chapel Hill, N.C., 1940) is a classic, the tone of which has led some wags to suggest the title might better be *Stonewall Rode with Me,* while William Dorsey Pender's letters to his wife, edited by William Woods Hassler as *The General to His Lady* (Chapel Hill, N.C., 1966), convey a sense of the opposition among many men in the Army of Northern Virginia to a raid across the Potomac.

Two excellent monographs explore the Maryland campaign in detail—James V. Murfin's *The Gleam of Bayonets* (New York, 1965) and Stephen W. Sears's *Landscape Turned Red* (New York, 1983). Both Murfin and Sears grounded their narratives in substantial research (Sears was far more thorough in manuscript sources) and included plentiful maps (Murfin has the edge cartographically); Sears's prose far surpasses Murfin's in its ability to render difficult tactical movements understandable and to sweep the reader along from one part of the sprawling campaign to another. Two specialized studies are indispensable to anyone visiting the modern battlefield: William A. Frassanito's *Antietam: The Photographic Legacy of America's Bloodiest Day* (New York, 1978) discusses the impact of the photographs taken shortly after the battle and offers modern shots of the same views, while Jay Luvaas and Harold W. Nelson provide a handy guidebook larded with quotations from the *Official Records* in *The U.S. Army War College Guide to the Battle of Antietam* (Carlisle, Pa., 1987). A handsome pictorial treatment is by Ronald H. Bailey and the editors of Time-Life Books, *The Bloodiest Day: The Battle of Antietam* (Alexandria, Va., 1984).

Two biographies of George B. McClellan are necessary to any study of Antietam (four other full-length studies of McClellan have been published in the twentieth century). Stephen W. Sears sketches a man tormented by visions of enemies all around him who lacked the courage to commit his Army of the Potomac to decisive battle in *George B. McClellan: The Young Napoleon* (New York, 1988). Far more favorable to McClellan is Warren W. Hassler, Jr., in *George B. McClellan: Shield of the Union* (Baton Rouge, La., 1957), the title of which suggests the thrust of the author's argument. Good shorter treatments of the Federal commander are T. Harry Williams's critical *McClellan, Sherman, and Grant* (New Brunswick, N.J., 1962) and Joseph L. Harsh's more gentle estimate in "On the McClellan Go-Round" (*Civil War History* 19 [June 1973]: 101–18).

Douglas Southall Freeman's *Lee's Lieutenants: A Study in Command* (3 vols.; New York, 1942–44), is the most famous—and widely read—history of the Army of Northern Virginia (Freeman's *R. E. Lee: A Biography* [4 vols.; New York, 1934–35] offers an immensely detailed, and often biased, portrait of the Confederate chief). Learned, spacious, and written with considerable grace, *Lee's Lieutenants* has remained for nearly half a century the obvious place to begin a study of any of Lee's operations. Two multivolume works on the Army of the Potomac merit attention: Kennth P. Williams's exhaustive *Lincoln Finds a General* (5 vols.; New York, 1949–59) consistently points out McClellan's failures of character and leadership; Bruce Catton's Army of the Potomac Trilogy, of which the first volume, *Mr. Lincoln's Army* (Garden City, N.Y., 1952), deals with Antietam, matches the narrative power if not the scholarship of Freeman's work. Perhaps best of all the narrative histories is Shelby Foote's *The Civil War: A Narrative* (3 vols.; New York, 1958–74); its first volume allots a generous amount of space to the Maryland campaign.

Thoughtful insights into the stategic thinking on both sides in the late summer and fall of 1862 may be found in T. Harry Williams's *Lincoln and His Generals* (New York, 1952) and Herman Hattaway and Archer Jones's *How the North Won* (Urbana, Ill., 1983). Specialized monographs of value are D. P. Crook's *The North, the South, and the Powers 1861–1865* (New York, 1974), an efficient treatment of diplomatic questions, and a pair of books on the problem of desertion, Ella Lonn's *Desertion during the Civil War* (New York, 1928) and Georgia Lee Tatum's *Disloyalty in the Confederacy* (Chapel Hill, N.C., 1934).

These thirty-odd titles provide a wealth of material for anyone hoping to understand the crisis of September 1862 and the Maryland campaign. Readers who seek more information or other points of view can pursue leads suggested in the footnotes and bibliographies of these books.

Index

Meade, George G., 78, 80, 87
Mediation: possibility of international, 3–4
Mercier, Henri, 4
Mexico, 3
Michie, Peter S., 56, 60
Middletown Valley, 63, 64
Miles, Dixon S., 17–22, 24, 28–29, 31–34, 59, 62
Military activity: significance of, in the Civil War, viii–ix
Militia Act (July 17, 1862), 4
Miller's Cornfield, vii, 52–54, 67, 73. *See also* Pasture
Mitchell, Barton, 24
Mitchell, Mary Bedinger, 42–43
Morell, George, 70
Moses, Raphael, 49
Munford, Thomas T., 49

Nashville, 2
New Orleans, 2
New York Times, 33, 91
New York Tribune, 80
Nicholls, Francis R. T., 51
Nicodemus Heights, 53, 69, 81
North: antiwar sentiment in, 5
North Carolina regiments: desertion among, 45–46
Northrop, Lucius, 50

Palfrey, Francis W., 25, 44, 56, 60
Palmerston, Viscount, 3, 4, 92
Parham, William Allen ("Gus"), 48–49, 51
Pasture, 54
Paxton, E. F., 51
Pender, Fanny, 86
Pender, William Dorsey, 10, 45, 86
Pendleton, William Nelson, 9
Peninsula campaign: McClellan's failure in, viii, 2, 57, 64; Southern generals and, 9
Perryville, viii
Photography: and Antietam, 91
Pinkerton, Allan, 60
Piston, William Garrett, 11
Pleasant Valley, 19, 29, 31, 48, 61, 63, 71, 88
Pleasonton, Alfred, 60, 63, 71, 73, 78
Plundering: by Confederate troops, 11
Pollard, Edward A., 85
Pope, John, 3, 7, 12, 57, 67, 78, 87

Porter, Fitz John, 60, 73, 77, 89
Pryor, Roger A., 49

R. E. Lee: A Biography (Freeman), 89
Railroad Brigade, 17
Ramseur, S. Dodson, 51
Randall, James Ryder, 37, 38
Randolph, George Wythe, 91
Rappahannock Station, 55
Reid, Whitelaw, 90
Reno, Joseph, 58, 62, 64
Republican party, 4, 5, 84, 93–94; and McClellan, viii, 89
Richardson, Albert D., 80, 81, 87
Richardson, Israel B., 70, 71, 72
Richmond, 35, 88
Richmond Enquirer, 91
Ricketts, James B., 52–53
Ripley, Edward Hastings, 27, 28
Ripley, Roswell S., 49–50, 54
Rockbridge Artillery, 86
Rodes, Robert E., 48–51, 53
Russell, Charles H., 24
Russell, John (Lord), 3, 4, 92
Russia: governmental interest in Civil War, 3, 92

School House Ridge, 22, 25, 27, 32–33
Sears, Stephen, 62, 83
Second Manassas. *See* Manassas, second battle of
Sedgwick, John, 53, 69, 70, 71, 77
Seven Days, viii, 1, 3, 4, 46, 51, 55, 57
Seven Pines, viii, 48
Seward, William H., 7
Sharpsburg, 41. *See also* Antietam
Sheridan, Philip H., 83
Sherman, William T., viii, 1, 83
Sherrill, Eliakim, 21
Shiloh, 2
Shoes: of Confederate troops, 10, 11, 39, 41
Slavery, 7, 91–92
Slocum, Henry W., 62, 72
Smith, Edmund Kirby, 1, 7
Smith, William F. ("Baldy"), 71, 72
Solomon's Gap, 19, 21
South Mountain, 19, 25, 27, 29, 34, 47, 57, 62–64, 88
Special Orders No. 191. *See* Lost Orders

Starke, William E., 51

Stonewall Brigade, 43, 46, 51

Straggling: of Confederate troops, 10–11, 39, 41–46, 54, 85; as Lee's excuse, 44–45. *See also* Desertion

Stuart, J. E. B. ("Jeb"), 9, 31

Sumner, Edwin V. ("Old Bull of the Woods"): at Antietam, 53, 58, 63, 65, 67, 69–70, 72–73, 77–80

Sunken Road, vii, 49, 51, 53, 67, 70-72, 77

Swinton, William, 71, 82

Sykes, George, 71, 78

Taylor, Walter H., 86

Tennessee: desertion among regiments from, 46

Thomas, George H., 1

Thompson, David L., 42

Thouvenel, Antoine Edouard, 3

Times (London), 3

Toombs, Robert A., 49

Turner's Gap, 29, 48, 61, 62, 63, 67

Union troops: Eleventh Corps, 60; Fifth Corps, 60, 77, 78, 81; First Corps, 52–53, 58, 67, 69, 70, 81; Fourth Corps, 59; Indiana (27th), 24, 47; Maryland Cavalry (1st), 24; Massachusetts (6th), 5; Massachusetts (13th), 81; New Jersey (11th), 87; New York (9th), 42, 87; New York (39th), 28; New York (51st), 75; New York (115th), 33; New York (125th), 27, 28, 32; New York (126th), 21–22; New York Cavalry (8th), 28; Ninth Corps, 58; Ohio (32nd), 21; Ohio (60th), 33; Pennsylvania (51st), 75; Second Corps, 58, 67, 69, 70, 71; Sixth Corps, 59, 71, 81; Twelfth Corps, 58, 67, 69, 70, 72, 81, 86; U.S. Infantry (9th), 78; Vermont (9th), 27, 28

Vicksburg, vii, viii

Vietnam, viii

Virginia, 37; desertion rate of regiments from, 46

Virginia Military Institute, 27, 50

Walker, J. A., 54

Walker, John G., 22, 25, 27, 43, 47, 59, 69

Warren, G. K., 78

Washington, George, 4

Welles, Gideon, 88

West Woods, vii, 51, 53, 67, 70, 77

White, Julius, 22, 33

White's Ford, 1, 5

Wightman, Edward K., 87

Wilcox, Cadmus M., 50

Willcox, Orlando, 78

Williams, Alpheus S., 58, 86–87

Williams, T. Harry, 57, 82

Wilson, John M., 73

Wofford, William T., 54

Yorktown, 4

Contributors

Dennis E. Frye began studying the siege of Harpers Ferry during his youth in Pleasant Valley, Maryland. A graduate of Shepherd College, he has served as the historian at Harpers Ferry National Historic Park since 1979. Active as a tour guide and lecturer, he is the author of *Second Virginia Infantry* and *Twelfth Virginia Cavalry* in the "Virginia Regimental History Series." He is currently writing a book on Stonewall Jackson's siege of Harpers Ferry.

Gary W. Gallagher is a member of the Department of History at Pennsylvania State University. He has published widely on the Civil War, including *Stephen Dodson Ramseur: Lee's Gallant General*, and *Fighting for the Confederacy: The Personal Recollections of General Edward Porter Alexander*. He is presently at work on a biography of Jubal A. Early.

A. Wilson Greene holds degrees in American history from Florida State University and Louisiana State University. A fifteen-year veteran of the National Park Service, he serves as the staff historian at Fredericksburg and Spotsylvania National Military Park. He has published articles in a variety of historical journals and is the author of *J. Horace Lacy: The Most Dangerous Rebel of this County*.

Robert K. Krick was raised and educated in northern California and has lived in Virginia for two decades. He is the author of eight books on Confederate history, among them *Lee's Colonels* and *Parker's Virginia Battery*. His latest work, *Stonewall Jackson at Cedar Mountain*, has a publication date of 1990.